THE
SHEPHERD OF MAN

An Official Commentary
on the Sermon of Hermes Trismegistos

Resurrectio.

Contents: Part 1, The Sermon and Commentaries of
Hermes Trismegistos; Part 2, The Origin of
Civilization; Atlanteans; Mayas; Akkadians;
Chaldeans; Egyptians; Nagas; Aryan Invasion.

A.S. Raleigh

ISBN 1-56459-493-9

DEDICATION

To that noble body of students, who are ever searching for the Truth beneath the symbol, who have devoted the greater portion of their lives to the Quest for the Hidden Wisdom, the true Knights of the Grail, this work is lovingly dedicated, with the hope that its perusal may aid them in the realization of their Quest.

THE AUTHOR.

CONTENTS

PART TWO.

The Origin of Civilization.

PREFACE

The Shepherd of Men is the Egyptian account of the Creation. We might in a certain sense term it the Egyptian Genesis. At the same time it must be borne in mind that it deals with the Genesis of the Gods as well as with that of the Universe. It is in fact the Kosmogony, Theogony, and the Anthropology of the Egyptian Secret Brotherhood. Any one reading the Sermon must at all times bear this in mind. We have here a very connected and very thorough account of the descent of the Spirit into Matter, as well as the descent of the Anthropos into Nature and the resultant engendering of individual human existence. The Sermon presents to us the clearest, and the most accurate, as well as the most thorough of all the extant accounts of the Genesis of life. It is at once scientific, philosophical and deeply religious. It is at the same time mystical and also very practical. It is the Theogony, Kosmogony and Anthropology of the Hidden Wisdom. This being the case, none but an Epopt could possibly furnish the Esoteric Key of the Sermon to the public. In times past, this Esoteric Key has been withheld from the public; but there has been so much erroneous teaching on the subjects treated in the Sermon that we have come to the conclusion that the only way in which this misinformation can be counteracted is to give the truth to the public. For this reason, I and my brother Epoptae have come to the conclusion that the time has come in which the Shepherd of Men must be unsealed. Inasmuch as the Mystery of God-the-Mind has been introduced into the Sermon, and in fact, plays the major role, it became evident that this unsealing of the Sermon must be done by an Initiate of that Mystery. As none of our Egyptian Brethren are Initiates of this Mystery, and as this Cultus is identical with the Cultus of the Heart of Heaven, among the Toltecs it was determined that the undersigned, being the High Priest of the Heart of Heaven, was the most desirable one to undertake the task. For this reason I was directed to write this Commentary on the Shepherd of Men.

Owing to my position in the Hierarchy, I am the one person on the earth today who can speak with absolute authority with reference to the subject matter of this Sermon. All that is contained in this Commentary is absolutely authoritative, and in it will be found the perfect key to the Esoteric Meaning of the Sermon. Any interpretation that may differ with the following in the slightest degree is, to the extent of such difference, erroneous.

In order to show the unity of the Hidden Wisdom throughout the world, it was necessary that we show that they had all received it from one common source. As there has been much dispute as to the source of this Wisdom, it became necessary that we should show the real truth as to the avenue through which this Hidden Wisdom spread over the world. To do this, it became necessary that we show who the people were who perpetuated the Hidden Wisdom. We have done this by showing that Atlantis was the source of the Hidden Wisdom, as well as of the civilization; that it passed to Egypt, Akkadia, Chaldea, India and Persia, by way of Yucatan, and that the Mayas were the ones who gave it to the world. We have shown that they did this through their colonization of those countries. The result of this is that we are able to see at a glance that it is through the despised American Indians that the world has received all of its Culture, Civilization and Wisdom. Where is it to be searched for at the present time? Among the people who gave it to the world in the first place. It is in the Indian Medicine Lodge that we find the Ancient Mysteries carried down to date. Look not in India or Persia for the Mysteries, but search in America, but above all in Mexico, and if the Gods bless you, there will you find them in all of their ancient purity. The reader will find the authentic history of the migrations of the Atlantians, and the work which they did for the extension of civilization. With these words we cast our little book upon the sea of human life.

HACH-MACTZIN EL DORADO CAN.

Chicago, Ill., March 15th, 1916.

The Shepherd of Men

(Text: Thrice Greatest Hermes,
G. R. S. Mead.)

———

TEXT.

1. It chanced once on a time my mind was meditating on things that are, my thought was raised to a great height, the senses of my body being held back—just as men are who are weighed down with sleep after a fill of food, or from fatigue of body.

Methought a Being more than vast, in size beyond all bounds, called out my name and saith: What wouldst thou hear and see, and what hast thou in mind to learn and know?

2. And I do say: Who art thou?
He saith: I am Man-Shepherd, Mind of all masterhood; I know what thou desirest and I'm with thee everywhere.

3. [And] I reply: I long to learn the things that are, and comprehend their nature, and know God. This is, I said, what I desire to hear.

He answered back to me: Hold in thy mind all thou wouldst know, and I will teach thee.

4. E'en with these words His aspect changed, and straightway, in the twinkling of an eye, all things were opened to me, and I see a Vision limitless, all things turned into Light—sweet, joyous [Light]. And I became transported as I gazed.

But in a little while Darkness came settling down on part [of it], awesome and gloomy, coiling in sinuous folds, so that methought it like unto a snake.

And then the Darkness changed into some sort of a Moist Nature, tossed about beyond all power of words, belching out smoke as from a fire, and groaning forth a wailing sound that beggars all description.

[And] after that an outcry inarticulate came forth from it, as though it were a Voice of Fire.

5. [Thereon] out of the Light—a Holy Word *(Logos)* descended on that Nature. And upwards to the height from the Moist Nature leaped forth pure Fire; light was it, swift and active, too.

The Air, too, being light, followed after the Fire; from out the Earth-and-Water rising up to Fire so that it seemed to hang therefrom.

But Earth-and-Water stayed so mingled each with other, that Earth from Water no one could discern. Yet were they moved to hear by reason of the Spirit-Word *(Logos)* pervading them.

6. Then saith to me Man-Shepherd: Didst understand this Vision, what it means?

Nay; that *shall* I know, I said.

That Light, He said, am I, thy God, Mind, prior to Moist Nature which appeared from Darkness; the Light-Word *(Logos)* [that appeared] from Mind is Son of God.

What then? say I.

Know that what sees in thee and hears is the Lord's Word *(Logos)*; but Mind is Father-

God. Not separate are they the one from other; just in their union [rather] is it Life consists.

Thanks be to Thee, I said.

So, understand the Light [He answered] and make friends with it.

7. And speaking thus He gazed for long into my eyes, so that I trembled at the look of Him.

But when He raised His head I see in Mind the Light, [but] now in Powers no man could number, and Cosmos grown beyond all bounds, and that the Fire was compassed round about by a most mighty Power, and [now] subdued had come unto a stand.

And when I saw these things I understood by reason of Man-Shepherd's Word (Logos).

8. But as I was in great astonishment He saith to me again: Thou didst behold in Mind the Archetypal Form whose being is before beginning without end. Thus spake to me Man-Shepherd.

And I say: Whence then have Nature's elements their being?

To this He answer gives: From Will of God [Nature] received the Word (Logos), and gazing on the Kosmos Beautiful did copy it, making herself into a Kosmos, by means of her own elements and by the births of souls.

9. And God-the-Mind, being male and female both, as Light and Life subsisting, brought forth another Mind to give things form, who, God as he was of Fire and Spirit,

formed Seven Rulers who enclose the Kosmos that the sense perceives. Men call their ruling Fate.

10. Straightway from out the downward elements God's Reason *(Logos)* leaped up to Nature's pure formation, and was at-oned with the Formative Mind; for it was co-essential with it. And Nature's downward elements were thus left reason-less, so as to be pure matter.

11. Then the Formative Mind ([at-oned] with Reason), he who surrounds the spheres and spins them with his whirl, set turning his formations, and let them turn from a beginning boundless unto an endless end. For that the circulation of these [spheres] begins where it doth end, as Mind doth will.

And from the downward elements Nature brought forth lives reason-less; for He did not extend the Reason *(Logos)* [to them]. The Air brought forth things winged; the Water things that swim, and Earth-and-Water one from another parted, as Mind willed. And from her bosom Earth produced what lives she had, four-footed things and reptiles, beasts wild and tame.

12. But All-Father Mind, being Life and Light, did bring forth Man co-equal to Himself, with whom He fell in love, as being His own child; for he was beautiful beyond compare, the Image of his Sire. In very truth, God fell in love with His own Form; and on him did bestow all of His own formations.

13. And when he gazed upon what the Enformer had created in the Father, [Man] too

wished to enform; and [so] assent was given him by the Father. Changing his state to the formative sphere, in that he was to have his whole authority, he gazed upon his Brother's creatures. They fell in love with him, and gave him each a share of his own ordering.

And after that he had well-learned their essence and had became a sharer in their nature, he had a mind to break right through the Boundary of their spheres, and to subdue the might of that which pressed upon the Fire.

14. So he who hath the whole authority o'er [all] the mortals in the cosmos and o'er its lives irrational bent his face downward through the Harmony, breaking r i g h t through its strength, and showed to downward Nature God's fair Form.

And when she saw that Form of beauty which can never satiate, and him who [now] possessed within himself each single energy of [all seven] Rulers as well as God's [own] Form, she smiled with love; for 'twas as though she'd seen the image of Man's fairest form upon her Water, his shadow on her Earth.

He in his turn beholding the form like to himself, existing in her, in her Water, loved it and willed to live in it; and with the will came act, and [so] be vivified the form devoid of reason.

And Nature took the object of her love and wound herself completely round him, and they were intermingled, for they were lovers.

15. And this is why beyond all creatures on

the earth man is twofold; mortal because of body, but because of the essential Man immortal.

Though deathless and possessed of sway o'er all, yet doth he suffer as a mortal doth, subject to Fate.

Thus, though above the Harmony, within the Harmony he hath become a slave. Though male-female, as from a Father male-female, and though he's sleepless from a sleepless [Sire], yet is he overcome [by sleep].

16. Therefore [I say: Teach on], O Mind of me, for I myself as well am amorous of the Word *(Logos)*

The Shepherd said: This is the mystery kept hid until this day.

Nature embraced by Man brought forth a wonder, oh so wonderful. For as he had the nature of the Concord of the Seven, who, as I said to thee [were made] of Fire and Spirit —Nature delayed not, but immediately brought forth seven "men," in correspondence with the natures of the Seven, male-female and moving in the air.

Thereon [I said]: O Shepherd, ... for now I'm filled with a great desire and long to hear; do not run off.

The Shepherd said: Keep silence, for not as yet have I unrolled for thee the first discourse *(Logos)* .

Lo! I am still, I said.

17. In such wise then, as I have said, the generation of these seven came to pass. Earth was as woman, her Water filled with longing;

ripeness she took from Fire, spirit from Aether. Nature thus brought forth frames to suit the form of Man.

And Man from Life and Light changed into soul and mind,—from Life to soul, from Light to mind.

And thus continued all the sense-world's parts until the period of their end and new beginnings.

18. Now listen to the rest of the discourse *(Logos)* which thou dost long to hear.

The period being ended, the bond that bound them all was loosened by God's Will. For all the animals being male-female, at the same time with man were loosed apart; some became partly male, some in like fashion [partly] female. And straightway God spake by His Holy Word *(Logos)* :

"Increase ye in increasing, and multiply in multitude, ye creatures and creations all; and man that hath Mind in him, let him learn to know that he himself is deathless, and that the cause of death is Love, though Love is all."

19. When He said this, His Forethought did by means of Fate and Harmony effect their couplings and their generations founded. And so all things were multiplied according to their kind.

And he who thus hath learned to know himself, hath reached that Good which doth transcend abundance; but he who, through a love that leads astray, expends his love upon his body,—he stays in Darkness wandering, and suffering through his senses things of Death.

20.   What is the so great fault, said I, the ignorant commit, that they should be deprived of deathlessness?

Thou seem'st, he said, O thou, not to have given heed to what thou heardst. Did not I bid thee *think?*

Yea, do I think, and I remember, and therefore give Thee thanks.

If thou didst think [thereon], [said He], tell me: Why do they merit death who are in Death?

It is because the gloomy Darkness is the root and base of the material frame; from it came the Moist Nature; from this the body in the sense-world was composed; and from this [body] Death doth the Water drain.

21.   Right was thy thought, O thou! But how doth "he who knows himself go unto Him," as God's Word *(Logos)* hath declared?

And I reply: the Father of the universals doth consist of Light and Life, and from Him Man was born.

Thou sayest well, [thus] speaking. Light and Life is Father-God and from Him Man was born.

If then thou learnest that thou *art* thyself of Life and Light, and that thou [only] *happen'st* to be out of them, thou shalt return again to Life.

Thus did Man-Shepherd speak.

But tell me further, Mind of me, I cried,

how shall *I* come to Life again—for God doth say: "The man who hath Mind in him, let him learn to know that he himself [is deathless]."

22. Have not all men then Mind?

Thou sayest well, O thou, thus speaking, I, Mind, myself am present with holy men and good, the pure and merciful, men who live piously.

[To such] my presence doth become an aid, and straightway they gain gnosis of all things and win the Father's love by their pure lives, and give Him thanks, invoking on Him blessings, and chanting hymns, intent on Him with ardent love.

And ere they give the body up unto its proper death, they turn them with disgust from its sensations, from knowledge of what things they operate. Nay, it is I, the Mind, that will not let the operations which befall the body work to their [natural] end. For, being door-keeper, I'll close up [all] the entrances and cut the mental actions off which base and evil energies induce.

23. But to the Mind-less ones, the wicked and depraved, the envious and covetous and those who murder do and love impiety, I am far off, yielding my place to the Avenging Daimon, who, sharpening the fire, tormenteth him and addeth fire to fire upon him, and rusheth on him through his senses, thus rendering him the readier for transgressions of the law, so that he meets with greater torment; nor doth he ever cease to have desire for appetites inordinate, insatiately striving in the dark.

24. Well hast thou taught me all, as I desired, O Mind. And now, pray, tell me further of the nature of the Way Above as now it is [for me].

To this Man-Shepherd said: When thy material body is to be dissolved, first thou surrenderest the body by itself unto the work of change, and thus the form thou hadst doth vanish, and thou surrenderest thy way of life, void of its energy, unto the Daimon. The body's senses next pass back into their sources, becoming separate, and resurrect as energies; and passion and desire withdraw unto that nature which is void of reason.

25. And thus it is that man doth speed his way thereafter upwards through the harmony.

To the first zone he gives the Energy of Growth and Waning; unto the second [zone], Device of Evils [now] de-energized; unto the third, the Guile of the Desires de-energized; unto the fourth, his Domineering Arrogance, [also] de-energized; unto the fifth, Unholy Daring and the Rashness of Audacity, de-energized; unto the sixth, Striving for Wealth by Evil Means, deprived of its aggrandizement; and to the seventh zone, Ensnaring Falsehood, de-energized.

26. And then, with all the energizing of the Harmony stript from him, clothed in his proper Power, he cometh to that Nature which belongeth unto the Eighth, and there with those-that-are hymneth the Father.

They who are there welcome his coming there with joy; and he, made like to them that sojourn there, doth further hear the Powers who are above the Nature that belongs unto the Eighth, singing their songs of praise to God in language of their own.

And then they, in a band, go to the Father home; of their own selves they make surrender of themselves to Powers, and [thus] becoming Powers they are in God. This the good end for those who have gained Gnosis—to be made one with God.

Why shouldst thou then delay? Must it not be, since thou hast all received, that thou shouldst to the worthy point the way, in order that through thee the race of mortal kind may by [thy] God be saved?

27. This when He'd said, Man-Shepherd mingled with the Powers.

But I, with thanks and blessings unto the Father of the universal [Powers] was freed, full of the power He had poured into me, and full of what He'd taught me of the nature of the All and of the loftiest Vision.

And I began to preach to men the Beauty of Devotion and of Gnosis:

O ye people, earth-born folk, ye who have given yourselves to drunkenness and sleep and ignorance of God, be sober now, cease from your surfeit, cease to be glamoured by irrational sleep!

28. And when they heard, they came with one accord. Whereon I say:

Ye earth-born folk, why have ye given up yourselves to Death, while yet ye have the power of sharing Deathlessness? Repent, O ye, who walk with Error arm in arm and make of Ignorance the sharer of your board; get ye from out the light of Darkness, and take your part in Deathlessness, forsake Destruction!

29.   And some of them with jests upon their lips departed [from me], abandoning themselves unto the Way of Death; others entreated to be taught, casting themselves before my feet.

But I made them arise, and I became a leader of the Race towards home, teaching the words *(Logoi)* how and in what way they shall be saved.   I sowed in them the words *(Logoi)* of wisdom; of Deathless Water were they given to drink.

And when even was come and all sun's beams began to set, I bade them all give thanks to God.   And when they had brought to an end the giving of their thanks each man returned unto his own resting place.

30.   But I recorded in my heart Man-Shepherd's benefaction, and with my every hope fulfilled more than rejoiced.   For body's sleep became the soul's awakening, and closing of the eyes—true vision, pregnant with Good my silence, and the utterance of my word *(Logos)* begetting of good things.

All this befell me from my Mind, that is Man-Shepherd, Word *(Logos)* of all masterhood, by whom being God-inspired I came unto the Plane of Truth.   Wherefore with all my soul and strength thanksgiving give I unto Father-God.

31.   Holy art Thou, O God, the universals' Father.

Holy art Thou, O God, whose will perfects itself by means of its own Powers.

Holy art Thou, O God, who willeth to be known and art known by Thine own.

Holy art Thou, who didst by Word (Logos) make to consist the things that are.

Holy are Thou, of whom All-nature hath been made an Image.

Holy art Thou, whose Form Nature hath never made.

Holy art Thou, more powerful than all power.

Holy art Thou, transcending all pre-eminence.

Holy Thou art, Thou better than all praise.

Accept my reason's offerings pure, from soul and heart for aye stretched up to Thee, O Thou unutterable, unspeakable, Whose Name naught but the Silence can express.

32. Give ear to me who pray that I may ne'er of Gnosis fail; [Gnosis] which is our common being's nature; and fill me with Thy Power, and with this Grace [of Thine], that I may give the Light to those in ignorance of the Race, my Brethren and Thy Sons.

For this cause I believe, and I bear witness; I go to Life and Light. Blessed art Thou, O Father. Thy Man would holy be as Thou art holy, e'en as Thou gavest him Thy full authority [to be].

The Shepherd of Men

(Text: Thrice Greatest Hermes,
G. R. S. Mead.)

SECTION I.

1. It chanced once on a time my mind was meditating on things that are, my thought was raised to a great height, the senses of my body being held back—just as men who are weighed down with sleep after a fill of food, or from fatigue of body.

Methought a Being more than vast, in size beyond all bounds, called out my name and saith: What wouldst thou hear and see, and what hast thou in mind to learn and know?

2. And I do say: Who art thou?

He saith: I am Man-Shepherd, Mind of all masterhood; I know what thou desirest and I'm with thee everywhere.

3. [And] I reply: I long to learn the things that are, and comprehend their nature, and know God. This is, I said, what I desire to hear.

He answered back to me: Hold in thy mind all thou wouldst know, and I will teach thee.

4. E'en with these words His aspect changed, and straightway, in the twinkling of an eye, all things were opened to me, and I see a Vision limitless, all things turned into Light—sweet, joyous [Light]. And I became transported as I gazed.

But in a little while Darkness came settling

down on part [of it], awesome and gloomy, coiling in sinuous folds, so that methought it like unto a snake.

And then the Darkness changed into some sort of a Moist Nature, tossed about beyond all power of words, belching out smoke as from a fire, and groaning forth a wailing sound that beggars all description.

[And] after that an outcry inarticulate came forth from it, as though it were a Voice of Fire.

5. [Thereon] out of the Light—a Holy Word (*Logos*) descended on that Nature. And upwards to the height from the Moist Nature leaped forth pure Fire; light was it, swift and active, too.

The Air, too, being light, followed after the Fire; from out the Earth-and-Water rising up to Fire so that it seemed to hang therefrom.

But Earth-and-Water stayed so mingled each with other that Earth from Water no one could discern. Yet were they moved to hear by reason of the Spirit-Word (*Logos*) pervading them.

6. Then saith to me Man-Shepherd: Didst understand this Vision, what it means?

Nay; that shall I know, I said.

That Light, He said, am I, thy God, Mind, prior to Moist Nature which appeared from Darkness; the Light-Word (*Logos*) [that appeared] from Mind is Son of God.

What then? say I.

Know that what sees in thee and hears is the Lord's Word; but Mind is Father-God.

Not separate as they the one from other; just in their union [rather] is it Life consists.

Thanks be to Thee, I said.

So, understand the Light [He answered] and make friends with it.

Commentary.

In the first place, we must understand the relationship subsisting between Hermes and Man-Shepherd. Hermes or Thoth, has been stated in former writings, as Kosmic Thought. Call to mind the former instruction with reference to Divine Reason or Primordial Ideation. The first manifestation of the Ultimate Spirit is in the form of Pure Spiritual Ideation, Ideation per se. This Ultimate Spiritual Ideation which manifests itself as Divine Love and Divine Will, and which is all back of the Creative Word, the Heart that Thinks, or Divine Thought, as is here called Man-Shepherd, Mind of all masterhood, for it is the Ultimate Mind. This is in reality that which is anterior to all Manifestation. This is what we might call Super-Kosmic Mind. Hermes is Kosmic Thought; that is, the reflection of this Super-Kosmic Mind or Spiritual Ideation in the Kosmic Energy or Akasa, becoming the Manifest Logos, or what in the Orient is called the Buddh, hence Hermes is the Manifestation or Emanation of Ultimate Mind.

Our Sermon represents Hermes, or Kosmic Thought, being instructed by Spiritual Ideation, or ultimate Mind. Mind is here the Master, and Kosmic Thought the Chela. This is quite proper, for Kosmic Thought is at all times the Mirror of Divine Mind, and reflects the Divine Thought in terms of Kosmic Thought. Therefore the Ideation of Divine Mind instructs Kosmic Thought, by becoming Manifest on the Plane of Kosmic Thought, and in that way regulating the Evolution of Kosmic Thought. Kosmic Thought being the Reflection in Kosmic Energy of Pure Spiritual Ideation, it follows that all the Thoughts of Thoth are imparted to Him by Primordial Mind.

In 1, we find that the mind of Hermes was meditating on the things that are; that is, Kosmic Thought was not directed to the aspects of the Manifest Universe, but rather to the Realities of its own plane, to the Ideal World rather than to the Sensible World. It was not directing Evolution in the World Without, but was rather turned inward in a process of Introspection, in Self-Contemplation of its own thoughts, the World of Ideas of Plato. In this process of Introspection, Kosmic Thought was raised to a great height; that is to say, it was dwelling on the very first beginnings of Kosmic Thought. This went to the extent that it was entirely removed from all the Manifest Universe, and was concentrated within the first beginnings of its own Thinking; that is, as a Hindoo would say, Hermes was in deep Samadhi. This often takes place, for otherwise it would not be possible for Kosmic Thought to be instructed by Divine Mind, and thus diverse Cycles of Spiritual Evolution would not be possible in the Kosmos.

This process of Introspection on the part of Kosmic Thought was carried to the extreme limit, and the result was the contacting of Spiritual Ideation, or Ultimate Mind. Having made the contact, the Divine Mind was Reflected in Kosmic Thought to the extent that the entire design and Modus of Kosmic Emanation was brought within the Radius of the Consciousness of Kosmic Thought. To understand this, we must bear in mind that Kosmic Thought is but the process of Kosmic Thinking; hence Kosmic Thought today is not what it was yesterday, it being ever changing; hence that which was the product of Kosmic Thought of one Epoch of Duration is not within the radius of Kosmic Thought of a later Epoch of Duration, hence Kosmic Thought requires to be Initiated from time to time by the Mind of all masterhood, or Spiritual Ideation.

Inasmuch as the things that are have been the product of a previous state of Kosmic Thought, the present state of Kosmic Thought—having been Evolved at a later period and being of a different order of Thought to that which Engendered them—is not able to fully understand their true nature. Because it is below the Plane of the Pure Spirit it cannot know that Spirit save as it is Reflected in its present State of Activity. Hermes therefore assumes a negative attitude with reference to Spiritual Mind and is ready to be taught by the latter, but to be in this way instructed he must hold in his mind all that he would know, that is, Divine Mind can only impart that to which Kosmic Thought is negative. When he is negative to Divine Mind, however, the latter is Mirrored in him, and thus he knows, or repeats in terms of Kosmic Ideation.

In 4 we are presented with an Apocalyptic Vision, which is in reality the Illumination of Kosmic Thought, or the Reflection in terms of Kosmic Thinking of that which was in the Conscious Memory of the Divine Mind, as having been the process of Emanative Creation. The Vision had to be explained to Kosmic Thought, for it was not sufficient that the original process should be repeated within His Thought, but also the Pure Thought of the Divine Mind must be Translated into terms of His Own Thought before he could understand, and thus manifest that Spiritual Consciousness in the form of the Consciousness of the Kosmos. This later form of Initiation is given in 6.

In the Apocalyptic Vision there first appeared within His Consciousness the original form of Limitless Light, which is the Original State of Primordial Mind, when it stood alone and there was not a Second. This is the Ultimate state when there has been nothing emanated and Spiritual Ideation is Concentrated within itself. This state of Primordial Light, which is Divine Mind, is followed by the Emanation of Darkness, which is the First Manifestation out of the Primordial Light of Ultimate Mind. This is the first beginning of Chaos which is later to become Kosmos. Nevertheless Nature as the Feminine Aspect of the Manifesting Energy has not as yet appeared. This Darkness is in reality the Primitive State of Kosmic Energy undifferentiated. This Chaotic Darkness which Emanated from Primordial Light enclosed the Light within itself, ensouling it, and then began the Spiral, undulatory, movement that was to ultimately Evolve a Kosmos. Thus it was that the Primordial Light was encompassed and enfolded by the Darkness of Primordial Chaos, and therefore Primordial Light is enclosed in Primeval Chaos; thus we have the Spirit within Nature; but at the same time the Spirit is also above Nature, for not all the Light was enfolded in the Darkness. Hence we have the Spirit or Primordial Mind in Manifestation and also is it Unmanifested as well.

In the Doctrine of the Two Truths, Water is at all times the Feminine Principle in Kosmos, just as Breath is the Masculine Principle. This being the case, it follows that the Moist Nature which appeared out of the Darkness of Primeval Chaos, was the Feminine aspect of that Chaos. Previous to this time Primordial Chaos was Sexless, but now out of it has proceeded the Feminine Aspect. This Feminine Principle is still perfectly Chaotic, but partakes of the nature of the

Feminine, hence the element of Moisture. At this stage Primary Moisture, the Primary Feminine element, is still united with Primeval Chaos, and the Travail which she endured in her efforts to free herself was terrific.

At last it cried to the Light, having become enamored of it, and realizing that its Master and Lord was in the Light. It cried to the Light to subdue it and reduce it to Order. The Feminine Moist Nature was expressing the Eternal Feminine in its longing for a master, that he might bring it into subjection to his will, and thus bring Order out of Chaos. From this longing there was enkindled within it the Fire of Love, and this Fire was expressed in a Voice, which reached upward to the Light.

5. In response to that Voice from the depths of the Moist Nature, there emanated from Primordial Light, or Divine Mind, the Holy Word of that Light, which is its counterpart on the Plane of the Moist Nature. This Holy Word of the Primordial Light or Mind is Son of God, or Son of Divine Mind. He is the Logos par excellence; that is, the Manifest Logos of the Kosmos that is to be. This is the Spoken Word of Primordial Divine Mind, which descends into the Realm of Nature to Manifest Primordial Mind. This Manifested Logos or Spoken Word, which is Kosmic Thought, descended upon Moist Nature and United with her, thus freeing her from Primeval Chaos, so that she was subdued and subjected to Reason, thus making the first beginnings of Kosmos. The result of this descending upon her of the Logos was the upward leaping from the Moist Nature of Pure Fire, the Fire of Love, which sprang up to meet the Logos, and they were made one. This fire leaped upward to the heights of the Manifested, and thus Primeval Chaos was transformed into Kosmic Order. Thus was born

out of Moist Nature the Kosmic Fire, with all the host of Fires.

The lowest aspect of the Moist Nature was Earth-and-Water in a mixed state, for they had not as yet become differentiated, Earth being the Physical Element, while Water, in this sense as the Lower Water, is the Astral Waters or Waters of Space. These were not separated but remained interblended in a sense. Therefore we have two Poles of Activity at this stage, Earth-and-Water representing the lower, and Fire the higher. By reason of this Polarity of action, there springs forth from the lower pole Earth-and-Water, or the still Chaotic aspect of the Moist Nature, Air, which follows after Fire and becomes next below it in the Kosmic Ordering of the Universe. Air being brought forth by the Moist Nature is her Second Son after Fire the First-Born. From the time of its birth from the Moist Nature, or the Great Mother, Air seemed to hang from Fire, they being so closely united.

Earth-and-Water were still so closely united and mingled one with the other that no one could discern the one from the other. Nevertheless the Logos, or Spoken Word of Spiritual Mind, was not only above but was also interpenetrating Earth-and-Water, and it was moved to hear; that is, was transformed by the activity of that Logos interpenetrating it. From this we realize that the Word was not simply confined to the Heights of the Kosmos, but interpenetrated every particle of it, even that which was still Chaotic in a measure.

In 6 the Lord's Word is the Manifesting aspect of the Primordial Mind; that is, the expression of that Mind in the Kosmos, hence the Spoken Word of Primordial Mind. It is this Manifestation of Mind within Kosmic Thought that renders it Intelligent, for that Manifestation is Kosmic

Ideation, the source of Kosmic Consciousness. While the Logos is the Manifestation of Mind, Mind is the Source of the Manifestation. Nevertheless they are not separate and independent the one of the other, but are in reality two Poles of the One Mind, and in this polarized Unity is it that all Life in the Komos consists; for it is through this Unity with Kosmic Thought that Spiritual Mind is able to Direct the Spiritual Will into the Kosmos and engender Kosmic Life.

The injunction to understand the Light, which is Mind, and make friends with it, means that it is only through the understanding of Primordial Light or Mind that Kosmic Thought will be enlightened, and that, through polarization with Mind, Kosmic Thought will be enriched and will Evolve to more perfect realization.

SECTION II.

7. And speaking thus He gazed for long into my eyes, so that I trembled at the look of Him.

But when He raised His head I see in Mind the Light, [but] now in Powers no man could number, and Cosmos grown beyond all bounds, and that the Fire was compassed round about by a most mighty Power, and [now] subdued had come unto a stand.

And when I saw these things I understood by reason of Man-Shepherd's Word *(Logos)*.

8. But as I was in great astonishment He saith to me again: Thou didst behold in Mind the Archetypal Form whose being is before beginning without end. Thus spake to me Man-Shepherd.

And I say: Whence then have Nature's elements their being?

To this He answer gives: From Will of God [Nature] received the Word *(Logos)* and gazing on the Kosmos Beautiful did copy it, making herself into a Kosmos, by means of her own elements and by the births of souls.

9. And God-the-Mind, being male and female both, as Light and Life subsisting, brought forth another Mind to give things form, who, God as he was of Fire and Spirit, formed Seven Rulers who enclose the Kosmos that the sense perceives. Men call their ruling Fate.

10. Straightway from out the downward elements God's Reason *(logos)* leaped up to Nature's pure formation, and was at-oned with the Formative Mind; for it was co-essential with it. And Nature's downward elements were thus left reason-less, so as to be pure matter.

11. Then the Formative Mind ([at-oned] with Reason), he who surrounds the spheres and spins them with his whirl, set turning his formations, and let them turn from a beginning boundless unto an endless end. For that the circulation of these [spheres] begins where it doth end, as Mind doth will.

And from the downward elements Nature brought forth lives reason-less; for He did not extend the Reason *(Logos)* [to them]). The Air brought forth things winged; the Water things that swim, and Earth-and-Water one from another parted, as Mind willed. And from her bosom Earth produced what lives she had, four-footed things and reptiles, beasts wild and tame.

12. But All-Father Mind, being Life and Light, did bring forth Man co-equal to Himself, with whom He fell in love, as being His own child; for he was beautiful beyond compare, the Image of his Sire. In very truth, God fell in love with His own Form; and on him did bestow all of His own formations.

Commentary.

In 7, after finishing the Instruction on the Vision of Creation, Mind—that is, Primordial Divine Mind—is said to gaze long into the eyes of Kosmic Thought. That is to say, the Primordial Mind is concentrated into a Positive Cur-

rent of Force flowing into Kosmic Thought, or
Kosmic Ideation, and there becoming manifested
as Kosmic Thought. It is in this way that Kosmic Thought is Initiated, in the same way as a
man may be through the Concentration of the
Hierophant, when he projects his own Consciousness into that of the Neophyte. The trembling on
the part of Kosmic Thought was the effect upon
the constitution of Kosmic Thought of this Influx
of Primordial Mind.

The raising of Mind's Head—that is, the ceasing
of this Concentration and the return of Primordial
Mind to its own Place—relieved Kosmic Thought
of this pressure, so that it could resume its own
activities and in that way become Conscious in
the normal manner. This illumination permitted
Kosmic Thought to see in Mind the Light—that
is, the Primordial Substratum of all Illumination,
the Principle of all Intelligence and the Eternal
Masculine Principle. At the same time this Light
had differentiated itself, or was rather in process
of differentiating itself, into innumerable Powers. That is to say, the Substance of all the Kosmic Powers is this Primordial Divine Light, which
has taken those diverse Forms or Modes of Activity. Not only was it the Light expressing itself
in the form of those Powers, but also it had become a Kosmos, and under this Form had expand-
ed from the first nucleus to an expanse beyond all
compare, and was in fact boundless. The Kosmos
is therefore nothing but the Mutation of Primordial Light. The Fire is the first state of the Ordered Kosmos, but out from this Fire there had
emanated another state of Kosmic Energy which
had become a most mighty Power. This Second-
ary Power, being subdued by the Power of Primordial Light acting upon it, had come unto a stand
—that is, it had become fixed in that new state.

Kosmic Thought was enabled to understand

all this by reason of the activity and operation of the Word, or Manifesting Reason of Primordial Mind, when it; that is to say, the Reason of Primordial Mind was acting upon the Specialized Substance of the Principle of Kosmic Ideation unto the end that it might be reproduced in terms of Kosmic Ideation, and thus the Consciousness of Primordial Mind be reproduced in terms of Kosmic Consciousness or Kosmic Thought; that is to say, Kosmic Thinking.

In 8, the great astonishment of Kosmic Thought indicates the slightly chaotic condition induced in that Kosmic Thinking Substratum by reason of the activity of Primordial Mind being brought to bear upon it. In Mind was beheld the Archetypal Form whose being is before beginning without end, for Primordial Mind is the Archetype of all that is or ever shall be. In Primordial Mind there is present the perfect structure that is to be externalized in the Universe, therefore it is the Archetype of all that is or is to be. Not only is it the Archetype, but it is also the Archetypal Form of all. Primordial Mind is in reality a perfect Kosmos, lacking nothing to make it complete, and in fact Evolution in the outward Universe is in proportion as it approaches the realization of this Primordial Kosmos, which is Perfection in itself. This Archetypal Form, which is the Pattern of all things in the Kosmos, not only of all things that are now manifesting, but of all that have manifested in the past, and that will yet manifest in the future, for it is the Pleroma (Fullness) that is only partially manifested in the Outer Kosmos of Nature at any one time or state of Evolution, is before endless beginning. Beginning is here used in the sense of the Process of the Ever Becoming, or the Indivisibility of Duration. It is that Process or originating Beginnings in the Process of Evolving Life. It is the Process of Engendering New Beginnings in **an** endless sequence. Beginning without end is therefore the perpetual process of Creative Evolution, dependent upon the Living, Self-Evolving, Self-Conscious Principle in Nature, which gives to us the Perpetual Generation, and Regeneration of the Universe through the Great Mother Essence of Nature. This beginning without End is a state subsequent to the Archetypal Form presented in Primordial Mind, and is in fact the expression of the latter through the Substance and Energy of the Manifested Kosmos. Nature is but the Externalization or outward Manifestation of the Archetypal Kosmos in Primordial Mind and follows it in every detail, though never realizing its Fullness.

As this is the case with the Manifested Kosmos as a Unity, with the Kosmic Substratum of all Nature's Elements, whence comes the being of those Elements in their differentiated state? In other words, given a Primordial Divine Unity, which manifests a Kosmical Unity, whence comes Diversity out of that Unity? In this we have propounded to us the great question which has shook the very foundations of philosophy, and which none but an Epopt of the highest attainments has ever been able to answer: given the Absolute Unity, without a second Principle, whence comes Relativity? This question Kosmic Thought is unable to answer, for the simple reason that the cause of relativity is not inherent in the Kosmos, but is to be found only in Primordial Divine Mind.

The answer is from Will of God. To understand this it is essential that one should understand the Essence of the Will of God. When Primordial Ideation has engendered within the Energy of Primordial Mind a Positive or Centrifugal Current of Force, flowing outward in Self-Expression, that Current of Primordial Mind Force is the Primordial Will, or the Divine Fiat,

which is at the same time but the Positive Pole of
Divine Mind. This Primordial Will being engendered by Divine Ideation is the Outflowing of Idea-
tion; and hence of all the Ideas engendered by that
Ideation; hence while it expresses the Unity of the
Divine Ideation, it at the same time expresses the
Particularity of the Diverse Ideas of the Divine
Ideator, thus manifesting a Unity which is but
the Synthesis of the Paticularity inherent in the
original Unity. It is thus a Unity which is the
Pleroma (Fullness) of Infinite Diversity. Thus
the Will of God acts both as a Unity and at the
same time as Infinite Diversity of Will Force.
When this Will Force energizes Kosmos the Diversity of its Will Forces awakens a corresponding Diversity of Energies within that Kosmic
Substratum, engendering a diversity of activities
which in turn engenders from that Kosmic Substance the Diversity of Nature's Elements.
Whereas, in the Primordial Mind and Will the
Unity was dominant, in the Kosmic Manifestation
the diversity becomes visible, while the Unity lies
hidden. Thus it is that Divine Will, while a Unity, engenders Kosmic Diversity by reason of its
own Dynamic Action.

Nature is the Self-Evolving, Self-Creative Process of Kosmic Energy-Substance, the Feminine
Principle or Moist Nature. She receives within
her own Essence the Word, or Manifestating Intelligence of the Primordial Mind, and as a result her Substance is transformed by the Dynamic
Action of that Word, she being perfectly Static
under its action. This word, becoming the Masculine Counterpart of the Moist Nature, is the
Intelligence of Kosmos, or rather of that Substratum which is to engender Kosmos. The
Logos, being the Positive or Masculine Correspondence of the Feminine Nature, caused it to
move in accordance with the Primordial Kosmos
of Divine Mind, and in that way to copy or re-

produce it within her own Substance and thus
make herself into a Kosmos, the exact duplicate
or Correspondence of that Divine Kosmos. To
understand this we must bear in mind the Essence
of Kosmos. Kosmos is in the first place a Picture. It is, when applied to the Universe, a Picture of the Universe—that is, of the Universal
Order. It is not so much, however, a picture of
something that is as it is of something that is to
be. In other words, Kosmos is first of all an
Ideal Picture in Divine Mind. This Picture in
the Divine Imagery, which contains within itself
all the elements of Universal Order, for it is the
Active Unity of Divine Ideation, is reflected in the
Mirror of Nature, and there being reproduced,
becomes no longer a Subjective Picture in the
Divine Consciousness, but is Objectivized in the
Substance of Nature, talking Form. Thus the
Divine Kosmos becomes the Negative of the Natural Kosmos which acts as the Positive of that
First Kosmos or Picture. The Primordial Kosmos is a Picture in Divine Consciousness, while
the Second Kosmos is that same Picture taking
Active Form, and hence the one is the Ideal Kosmos, while the other is the Actual Kosmos, though
not the Sensible Kosmos, for it is not approach-
able through the Senses, but only through the
Reason. Nature actualized the First Kosmos by
causing her Specialized Elements to externalize
the particular Attributes of that First Kosmos,
and also through the giving birth to diverse souls,
who Individualized the diverse aspects and modes
of the Ideal Kosmos. In this way was she able
to Duplicate in Herself the First Kosmos.

In 9, God-the-Mind is, of course, Primordial
Divine Mind. This Divine Substratum of all there
is, or is to be, is in its own Esse male and female
both. This male and female Essence subsists in
Light and Life, Light being the Esse of Intelligence and the Essence of Illumination, while Life

is the Energy through which Intelligence is perpetually being expressed. At the same time they are not two in a state of separateness, but rather the two poles of Unity acting simultaneously. Life is the Substance of Light, and Light is the Energy of Life. This two-fold Divine Mind, subsisting in Light and Life, by reason of its Energizing Nature caused the awakening within her substance of Intelligent Activity, thus engendering another Mind, within Nature's own Esse. Thus was born the Mind of Nature or Kosmos. This Kosmic Mind is identical with Kosmic Thought, and being engendered through the action of Divine Mind upon Nature, is the exact correspondence of that Higher Mind, but operative upon the Plane of the Actual or Second Kosmos. Therefore it is also double-sexed as Light and Life. This Kosmic Mind, by reason of its double action as Light and Life, causes the mutations of Nature Substance to be in accordance with its Thinking, and in this way to so transform that Nature Substance into diverse forms, the expression of its Thinking. Thus it is for the purpose of engendering things by giving them form. In this Formative Mind the Light becomes the Kosmic Fire and the Life becomes Spirit, the Syzygy of the Fire. The Fire and Spirit of the Formative Mind, acting upon Nature, caused her to bring forth the Seven Rulers. All Universal Action is Septiform, and hence the Fire and Spirit of the Formative Mind acts through a Sevenfold Impulse. This Sevenfold Impulse of the Formative Mind acts upon the Kosmic Substance and the transforming Energy of Nature, and thus Nature specializes Seven distinct Modes of Formative Energy, each of which acts upon the Natural Substance in its own peculiar way, thus tending to engender that special form of Creative Activity. These are the Seven Creative Fires, or the Seven Creative Spirits, called the Gucumatz by

the Mayas and the Quiches. Through the com-
bined action of these Seven Creative Fires the
Sensible Kosmos was engendered, therefore they
are said to enclose it. They enclose it in the
sense that it is in and through their united action
that the Sensible Kosmos subsists, they being
the Formative Agents that are ever forming and
transforming it. As their Formative Action is,
so is the sensible Form of the Kosmos at any
given moment of Duration. From this Formative
Action of the Seven Rulers proceeds all those
specialized Modes of Energy which constitute
what are called the Laws of Nature, and the Synthetic Action of which determines the Course of
Creative Evolution in the Sensible Kosmos, thus
giving to Sensuous Nature that determinate
Trend which is termed Fate or Destiny.

In 10, God's Reason or Logos is the Reason that
had previously descended into Nature and had
permeated her entire Being. This Reason was
present in the entire extension of Nature. It now
leaped up to Nature's Pure Formation—that is,
to the Creative Evolutionary Principle, or the
Great Mother—and was atoned with the Formative Mind, for it was co-essential with it. This
point will require a bit of elucidation. The Logos
is not the same as the Formative Mind, for they
are in reality the two aspects of Kosmic Thought.
The Formative Mind is that aspect of Kosmic
Thought that acts upon the Substance and Energy of Nature, and thus determines her Formative Activity, giving rise in this way to the ever-
changing Form of the Sensuous Kosmos. It is
therefore the Intelligence expressing itself
through the Great Mother and directing the Evolution of Form. It is, in fact, the Mind engendering Creative Evolution. The Logos, on the other
hand, is that aspect of Kosmic Thought which
has nothing to do with the process of Creative
Evolution, or the engendering of Form, but which

concerns itself with the Speculative aspect of Kosmos. The Formative Mind is the Practical Reason of the Kosmos, while the Logos is its Pure Reason. The Formative Mind is concerned with the continual evolution of the form of the Sensible Kosmos, while the Logos is concerned with the Spiritual Evolution of the Real Kosmos—that is, the Super-Sensible Kosmos. It is this Logos that is ever in touch with Primordial Mind. It is through the Logos that Kosmic Thought was able to be instructed by Man-Shepherd, it is through the Formative Mind that He is able to impart this Instruction to the Kosmos. For this reason we are to understand that in the Ecstacy described in the opening of the Sermon, Kosmic Thought was drawn out of the Formative Mind and was centered in the Logos aspect. And yet this Reason and the Formative Mind are not two, but the two poles of one Kosmic Mind. They are both of one Essence, being the two poles of manifestation of that Essence.

As a result of this Polarization of Reason with the Formative Mind Nature's downward elements —that is, all that proceeded from the Seven Rulers—having the Reason withdrawn from them, were left reason-less. They no longer ensouled the Reason, which therefore could not act from within them direct, but could henceforth act only mechanically, under the impulse of the Formative Mind. Reason had left the region of Formation and had gone to its own place, between Primordial Mind and the Formative Mind, to be the Intermediatory Principle between the two. Therefore the elements of the Sensuous Kosmos became pure matter in the sense that they were devoid of Reason. Thus was engendered the Material Universe in the true sense.

The Formative Mind being now at-oned with Reason, and acting in conjunction with it, this

Formative Mind, that surrounds or contains the spheres or realms of the material Kosmos within itself and spins them with its whirl or spiral motion, we are told in 11, set turning his formation—that is, the Material Kosmos, formed by reason of its action on the Formative Process. This means the engendering of the spiral motion in the perpetual mutations of the Sensible Kosmos. The beginning boundless means an unlimited number of beginnings—that is, there were engendered within these realms of matter tendencies innumerable, each one conditioning the mode of action of matter. This relates to the beginnings of the diverse aspects of Creative Evolution. Each tendency is reproduced in accordance with Creative Evolutionary Law, thus the end of a tendency is but its beginning again, the beginning being born out of the end and partaking of the fruitage of that which has thus ended. Therefore, that which begins is inherent in that which ends, hence the beginning is the end in a new aspect. This ending is a perpetual process, which is incessantly active at all times. Duration being Indivisible not only in time but also in aspect. This process of ending, being endless, just as the process of beginning is boundless, it is called an endless end. Through this process of Infinite Mutation, embodying a boundless beginning and an endless end, the Formative Mind maintains the spheres of the Sensible Kosmos in a perpetual spiral movement. Thus it is that Creative Evolution is the expression of the Formative Mind through matter. All this is but the expression of the Will, the Positive Dynamic Force of Formative Mind, which is ever externalizing itself through the form of the Material Kosmos.

Nature, as the Formative Process in the Substance and Energy of the Second Kosmos, acting upon the downward elements of the Sensible Kosmos, from them were engendered lives rea-

son-less. First of all they were engendered as
lives, or specialized Modes of Life; later these
lives were incorporated into forms, for the lives
were the specialized Modes of Energy and their
forms were the specialized forms of Substance.
The Reason having previously withdrawn from
those elements, the Formative Mind did not extend it to the lives that were formed of the material elements. Out of the Airy Principle were
engendered all winged creatures, they being the
specialized and individualized aspects of the Airy
principle. In the same manner the Watery Principle, being acted upon by the Formative Mind and
the Formative Vigor of Nature, engendered from
its own Energy and Substance all things that
swim therein, for they are but the specialized and
individualized forms of the Water. The Formative Mind now acted upon the compound or rather united form of Earth-and-Water so that they
parted one from the other and each became a
separate element. Earth now specialized her Life
Forces, so that they assumed the form proper to
them, thus engendering from the depths of the
Earth Principle all the forms of beasts both wild
and tame—that is, those that are now wild and
tame—each Family coming forth separate, and
all reptiles in like manner. Thus were engendered the entire irrational creation. They were all
the product of Formative Nature under the impulse of Formative Mind, acting independent of
Reason.

In 12, we depart from the work of Nature
and the Formative Mind and find All-Father
Mind—that is, the Primordial Spiritual Mind—
undertaking the work of Creation direct. The
Life and Light, or Intelligence and Living
Essence of Primordial Mind, being centered
the one into the other, did engender from
their own Essence Man. He being engendered from the Life and Light of Divine Mind was

co-equal to the Essence which was specialized
in him. Because this Man was the specialized Essence of Primordial Mind, and as such His
own child and His very Image, for he was the
Individualized aspect of that Universal Essence,
the Primordial Divine Mind fell in love with him,
and they were polarized the one with the other.
In this manner the Man became the Body of Divine Mind, or rather his Spiritual Form, in which
His Fullness was made manifest. This Man, however, must not be confused with the human. He
was not the Individual Man, but was rather the
Heavenly or Kosmical Man. This Heavenly Man
was the Specialized Mode of Manifestation of
Primordial Mind, and through this Mode was He
able to make His Own Pure Essence manifest in
Kosmos. It is here that we get the origin of the
concept of the Heavenly Man, or the Man par
excellence. He was the focal aspect of Primordial Spiritual Consciousness. He being the Form
of Primordial Divine Essence, that Essence fell
in love with him, and being continually drawn to
him, was poured into this Form, and in him was
manifested all the formations of the Divine Essence of Primordial Mind. This was not as in
a lower aspect, as was the case with the Logos,
but rather as being on a level with the Primordial
Mind. Thus did Primordial Mind become outwardly conscious in its Fullness in this Archetypal Heavenly Man. He was therefore set over
all the Mutations of Nature as well as the Formative Mind and even the Manifesting Logos. This
is the man that was set over the works of God's
Hand, not the later Human Man. This man was
therefore not of the Formative Sphere at all.
He was not part of the Second Kosmos, for he
was in fact the Manifest Form of the Primordial
Kosmos. We must not associate the First Man
with the concept of a Being in the ordinary sense
of the word, for He was not that in any sense

whatsoever, being in reality a Specialized Mode of the Primordial Spirit, rather than a Person. If the term Person be applied to Him at all, he was the Personality of Primordial Mind, while Primordial Mind in its Pure Esse was Impersonal. This Heavenly Man is the real Anthropos of the Gnosis and of all Hermetic Teaching. He, being the Individualized Intelligence of the Father, must be the channel through which the Universe below him is to be Individualized.

SECTION III.

13. And when he gazed upon what the En-former had created in the Father, [Man] too wished to enform; and [so] assent was given him by the Father. Changing his state to the formative sphere, in that he was to have his whole authority, he gazed upon his Brother's creatures. They fell in love with him, and gave him each a share of his own ordering.

And after that he had well-learned their es-sence and had became a sharer in their na-ture, he had a mind to break right through the Boundary of their spheres, and to subdue the might of that which pressed upon the Fire.

14. So he who hath the whole authority o'er [all] the mortals in the cosmos and o'er its lives irrational bent his face downward through the Harmony, breaking r i g h t through its strength, and showed to down-ward Nature God's fair Form.

And when she saw that Form of beauty which can never satiate, and him who [now] possessed within himself each single energy of [all seven] Rulers as well as God's [own] Form, she smiled with love; for 'twas as though she'd seen the image of Man's fairest form upon her Water, his shadow on her Earth.

He in his turn beholding the form like to himself, existing in her, in her Water, loved it and willed to live in it; and with the will came act, and [so] he vivified the form devoid of reason.

And Nature took the object of her love and wound herself completely round him, and they were intermingled, for they were lovers.

15. And this is why beyond all creatures on the earth man is twofold; mortal because of body, but because of the essential Man immortal.

Though deathless and possessed of sway o'er all, yet doth he suffer as a mortal doth, subject to Fate.

Thus, though above the Harmony, within the Harmony he hath become a slave. Though Male-female, as from a Father male-female, and though he's sleepless from a sleepless [Sire], yet is he overcome [by sleep].
Word [*Logos*].

16. Therefore [I say: Teach on], O Mind of me, for I myself as well am amorous of the

The Shepherd said: This is the mystery kept hid until this day.

Nature embraced by Man brought forth a wonder, oh so wonderful. For as he had the nature of the Concord of the Seven, who, as I said to thee [were made] of Fire and Spirit—Nature delayed not, but immediately brought forth seven "men," in correspondence with the natures of the Seven, male-female and moving in the air.

Thereon [I said]: O Shepherd, ... for now I'm filled with a great desire and long to hear; do not run off.

The Shepherd said: Keep silence, for not

as yet have I unrolled for thee the first discourse *(logos)*.

Lo! I am still, I said.

17. In such wise then, as I have said, the
generation of these seven came to pass. Earth
was as woman, her Water filled with longing;
ripeness she took from Fire, spirit from
Aether. Nature thus brought forth frames
to suit the form of Man.

And Man from Life and Light changed into
soul and mind,—from Life to soul, from Light
to mind.

And thus continued all the sense-world's
parts until the period of their end and new
beginnings.

18. Now listen to the rest of the discourse
(logos) which thou dost long to hear.

The period being ended, the bond that
bound them all was loosened by God's Will.
For all the animals being male-female, at the
same time with man were loosed apart; some
became partly male, some in like fashion
[partly] female. And straightway God spake
by His Holy Word *(Logos)*:

"Increase ye in increasing, and multiply in
multitude, ye creatures and creations all; and
man that hath Mind in him, let him learn to
know that he himself is deathless, and that
the cause of death is Love, though Love is
all."

Commentary.

In 13 the Archetypal Man, beholding the Kosmos created in the Father, that is, Mind or Primordial Ideation by the Enformer, or the Formative
aspect of Primordial Mind, and reflected in the

Second Kosmos, through the Formative Action of the Formative Mind, in his turn wished to enform, or give formative expression to the Ideal which was present in his own mind. The Father, or Primordial Mind, gave assent to the sense that there was reflected in him that Mind which was inherent in the Father, and thus, he was empowered to give formative expression to his thought. For the Archetypal Man was the Reflection of all the potencies of All-Father Mind Itself.

This desire on the part of the Archetypal Man changed his state to the formative sphere, in that it caused him to descend from the sphere of Pure Ideation into that of Formation, that is, into the region of the Formative Mind, which was henceforth under his dominance. in that it obeyed the impluse of his will. His Brother is the Formative Mind, and his Brother's creatures are the first creations of the Formative Mind. When they fell in love with him, the meaning is that all the Formative Modes, engendered by the Formative Mind were at-oned with the Archetypal Man, and being at-oned with him, they were under his control, for he was now the Positive Pole and they were the Negative Pole of action in that realm. Thus it was that they each gave him a share of their power for his own ordering, as he was now the directing intelligence for the Modes engendered by the Formative Mind. Not only was this true of the Modes of the Formative Mind, but also the Activities of the Formative Process that was directed by those Modes of the Formative Mind. In a word, from this time forth Man was Director of Creative Evolution, and hence Master of the Formative Mind.

As a result of this process, Man mastered the essences of those Formative Modes, and became a sharer in their nature, in the sense that He en-

souled all of those Modes and was in that sense
an Incarnation, if we might use such a term for
the Archetypal Man, of all the Formative Modes.
Next there grew up within him the thought to
break right through the Boundary of the spheres,
and in this way embody all the Formative Potency of the Formative Process of the Great
Mother, and likewise of the Seven Spheres of the
Seven Rulers, or the Gucumatz, thus becoming
Master of all Formation, and in this way subdue
the might of that Third Kosmos that was press-
ing on the Fire of the Formative Realm. In a
word, he was not content to be the synthesis of
all the world of formation, but he even aspired
to ensoul and dominate the Kosmic Form as well.

In 14 this Man who was the Individualized Form
of Primordial Mind, and hence the Manifest Form
of God the Mind, broke through in bond of the
Harmony of the Seven Rulers, thus becoming
Master of all those Seven Spheres, and coming in
touch with downward Nature. Thus was God's
fair Form brought into contact with the Third
Kosmos, or Downward Nature.

At this stage Man was not only the Individualized Form of Primordial Mind, but was also the
perfect synthesis of all the energies of the Seven
Rulers. In a word, he had become the Enformer
of all below, as well as the Pure Intelligence.
From this time forth the Image of the Man was
reflected in the Watery Realm of Nature, thus
transforming it into his Image, and likewise was
his Shadow cast upon the Earthy Element, so
that Nature became the Mirror of the Man. This
caused Nature to respond with love, so as to draw
Man into union with herself. It was the creation
of affinity between Nature and the Archetypal
Man, an Affinity that was destined to merge the
two completely into One.

When the Man beheld the reflection of his own

Form in the Water of Nature, he loved it, for he saw in it the reflection of himself, and resolved to live in it. Thus did man descend into the Image of himself, and vivify this form devoid of Reason, with his own power and Mind. Thus it was no longer his Reflection but his very self that was present in the Water. Man now lived in the Water as his abiding Form.

Having descended into the Water of Nature, she responded with love, and wound herself about him, so as to make of him her soul, and to give him an abiding form through which his Mind and will might find expression. Thus was Archetypal Man enfolded in the realm of Nature, endowing her with the potentiality of Mind.

In 15 we find that this led to a dual nature in Man. That part which was above the boundary of Nature was still Immortal, and the abode of Pure Mind, but that which was enfolded in Nature was Mortal, as she was. In the Higher Realm of his being The Man was Master over all, yet his Natural Form is subject to Fate; for it is composed of Fate-dominated Nature and as such it cannot partake of the Super-Natural Power. However, we must bear in mind that this is still the One Man, the Anthropos, that we are speaking of. Individual Man had not as yet been produced.

He lives both above the Harmony, and within the Harmony of the Spheres and that portion of his being which is above the Harmony is Master of that Harmony, yet that portion of Him which is within the Harmony, being enclosed by it, is a slave to the Harmony which enfolds Him. He is therefore Master of all the Mutations of Nature, and at the same time in his Lower Nature, subject to these Mutations. Being the Perfect Form of Primordial Mind, which is male-female, he is also male-female, and being relatively Immortal and hence sleepless, yet in his Natural Form is he overcome by sleep, because of the fact that he is in this form subject to decay and exhaustion.

In 16 Kosmic Thought having reproduced all this is unable to follow the sequence farther, and must again return to Primordial Mind, being polarized with It in order that the rest of the sequence may be manifested in It. The amor of Kosmic Thought for the Logos, which is here the First Logos, or Word of Primordial Mind, was the force of Union between the two which caused Primordial Mind to be mirrored in Kosmic Thought.

Through the Union between the Archetypal Man and Nature, she being impregated by the sevenfold power of the Man, in whom were resident the full Concord of the Seven Creative Powers or Rulers, reflected in herself the Sevenfold Creative Power, and thus brought forth seven "men," corresponding to the Seven Powers, but pertaining to the realm of Nature. In a word, they were the reflection in Nature of the Seven Rulers of the Pure Abode of the Great Mother. These seven "men," being the Natural Counterpart of the Seven Rulers, were like them, male-female. As they were the sevenfold specialized forms of Her Airy Principle, they were the Seven Airs, just as their Archetypes are the Seven Fires. Thus were the Seven Fiery Rulers reflected in the Air of Nature. Hence are they said to float in the Air. Thus was born the Mind of Nature, or what is called Manus. This came forth as a result of the conjunction of the Archetypal Man with Irrational Nature, and thus was She endowed with Mind, albeit not the mind of Her Lord, but a reflection of that in Her own Air.

At this point Kosmic Thought is excited to the highest pitch at the disclosure, but as such activity would render it positive to Primordial Mind, it is stilled so that it may be receptive to the Motions of the Pure Mind, and then the following revelation is made concerning the farther operations of the Man in his relations to Nature.

In 17 Earth become as woman, that is, she is perfectly feminine and Negative to the Power of the Man, now operating through the mediums of the seven "men." They are having become the sevenfold form of her Air, or the Seven Airs, it is only through Her Water that they can operate. Her Water is filled with longing for the Men, that they may descend to its embrace. This longing drew down the Fire, so that it dried and ripened the Water, preparing it for its future function. From the Aether came the Spirit of Nature, and thus was the Water Ripened and Spiritualized, becoming the Astral Light. From this was brought forth the frames in which the Form of Man was to be Individualized into diverse men.

Because of Man's Amor for Nature, his form entered the Frames prepared for it, His Pure Life becoming soul, and the Light resident in Him becoming Mind. Thus were Life and Light Individualized into Individual Soul and Mind, and hence Man began the Inividual Life of the Humanity of the Astral World.

Hence it is thenceforth, in this particularity, that the Kosmic Man continues through all the Cycles of Life, for the Unity of the Kosmic Man was lost in the Particularity of His Manifestations in the diverse Frames prepared for him. This is the real beginning of the Human Race, though at this time they were of Watery Bodies, that is, pertaining to the Astral Region, not having as yet descended into Physical Incaration. They were still male-female, as were their Archetypes. There was a long period during which they continued in this state before the descent into the Earth Life.

In 18 we come to the end of this Watery Period wherein all life is Astral, and enter the Earthy Period of Etheric Life. Having entered that state, the Bond of Unity that held them as male-female was loosed by Will of God. That is, the dynamic power of the Divine Fiat acted upon all Nature unto the end that the two elements were tending to separateness. The masculinity and femininity resident in both the animals and the men was loosed apart, not suddenly but gradually, so that in the course of time some became partly male and other partly female. The meaning of this being that no one, either animal or man, is entirely male or female. The two sexes were still blended in all, but in different degrees of completeness, for the masculine is latent in the female and the feminine is latent in the male, the masculine overpowering the feminine in the male and the feminine overpowering the masculine in the female. Thus was developed what we term the male and the female, both in the animals and in man. From henceforth there were no longer male-female, but those relatively male and those relatively female.

When the separation into the two sexes had taken place they no longer found the opposite sex within themselves, but in another, and the arousing of the sex force within them sought its other pole in one of the opposite sex, and thus was born within them mutual sex desire, thus were they prompted to love for one of the other sex, and this love prompted them to seek their mate in another, and not in themselves as in times past. This led to the desire to propagate their kind through the sexual embrace. It is in this sense that they were told to increase and multiply. It was the working of the Divine Law within them which drove them together. Not only was this the case with the animals, but also with man. For man and woman being formed, they must needs seek each the other, and in this way fulfill the Law of Generation. At the same time man is to know that in his ultimate nature he is deathless, hence no man dies because of anything in his real nature, but because of a cause which he sets up within himself, apart from his true nature. Thus it is to be seen that death is no part of the regular order of human life, but is in the very nature of things, self-induced by the one who dies. The cause of death is love, that is, love between sexes. Man in the a-sexual state has within himself the potentialities of both sexes, and when those sex potentialities are equally developed they manifest the perfect male-female state. In this state of double-sexed life the two sexes are polarized, and the result is perpetual renewal or regeneration. In this way death is impossible, for the simple reason that the structure is continually reproduced. The renewal of the organism, which is the result of the interactivity of the dual sex forces within the soul and body, is the source of the essential deathlessness of man so long as he remains in this state. When the two sexes are separated they must be brought together again in order that they may be polarized within, and thus the work of regeneration commences. This being the case, it is evident that there is but one avenue through which this work can be brought into manifestation. The latent sex force must be awakened and developed to the point where it will be perfectly balanced with the dominant sex. To do this, one must be in a state of perpetual love with himself. That is to say, the dominant sex force must fall in love with the latent sex force, and through a process of perpetual love-making between the two, awakening of the latent sex force must be brought about. This being the case, if one falls in love with the opposite sex force as it is manifesting in another, this will prevent the awakening of the latent sex force within himself, and thus the process of regeneration cannot possibly begin so long as he loves one of the other sex. Thus it is that the cause of death is love. That is, love of one of the opposite sex, because it replaces the process of regeneration by the process of generation. Before regeneration can begin it is essential that all love between men and women must utterly cease, and be replaced by the love between the man and the woman within oneself. Thus it is to be seen that intersexual love is the cause of death, and every expression of it is another step in the way of death. It is only by awakening sexual love within oneself, between the two poles of his own nature, that this death-dealing process may be ended and the way of life be entered upon. This is accomplished through the restoration of the double-sexed nature of man and the polarization of the two forces within. Thus it is to be seen that death will only be overcome by the Androgyne Man; all men and women must die. Notwithstanding this death-dealing effect of love yet love is all. Love is the principle of Union, and therefore if rightly directed it will lead one into the highest realms, but when the love principle is operative between two different souls in the sexual sense it tends to curtail the unfoldment of each, and in time to tear asunder the two elements in each, so that it is found to be the Way of Death. All such relationships on whatever Plane are found to be unmixed evil, insofar as the effect on Life is concerned. It leads to death, and also to the prevention of all progress and evolution so far as the manifestation of the Deathless nature of the man through the bodily form is concerned. The question then is, how much of man is subject to the death-dealing effects of love? As much of him as is in love with a woman. All the principles that are in love with one of the opposite sex are doomed to dissolution. It is from this point of view that woman is said to be the cause of man's woe. It is not woman, but love of the opposite sex; but to the man this is most naturally expressed through the symbol of woman, for it is with woman that he is in love, and he can never be saved from death and enter the Plane of Regeneration so long as he loves her. At the same time it would be just as appropriate for woman to say that it is man that has doomed her, for he is the natural symbol of love between the sexes so far as she is concerned, and she can only be saved by ceasing to love him, and finding her man within herself. In the case of either man or woman the beloved must be sought and found within and not without. This is the true marriage of the soul and the one way of redemption.

Through love between the sexes was begun the workings of the Law of Generation, which leads to death, and through this the Androgyne love, with its Law of Regeneration leading unto life, was shut off and has never been found in its entirety even to this day. At the same time we wish it understood that in those rare instances where there are presented to us persons embodying the double-sexed nature they are not freaks of nature, but are rather instances in which the original form of man is striving to reproduce itself, and the nearer the two sexes approach the point of balance the nearer human perfection is the one in whom this blending is found. Men and women are only half souls or half men, but the Androgyne is perfect.

SECTION IV.

19. When He said this, His Forethought did by means of Fate and Harmony effect their couplings and their generations founded. And so all things were multiplied according to their kind.

And he who thus hath learned to know himself, hath reached that Good which doth transcend abundance; but he who, through a love that leads astray, expends his love upon his body,—he stays in Darkness wandering, and suffering through his senses things of Death.

20. What is the so great fault, said I, the ignorant commit, that they should be deprived of deathlessness?

Thou seem'st, he said, O thou, not to have given heed to what thou heardst. Did not I bid thee *think?*

Yea, do I think, and I remember, and therefore give Thee thanks.

If thou didst think [thereon], [said He], tell me: Why do they merit death who are in Death?

It is because the gloomy Darkness is the root and base of the material frame; from it came the Moist Nature; from this the body in the sense-world was composed; and from this [body] Death doth the Water drain.

21. Right was thy thought, O thou! But how doth "he who knows himself go unto Him," as God's Word [Logos] hath declared?

And I reply: the Father of the universals

doth consist of Light and Life, and from Him Man was born.

Thou sayest well, [thus] speaking. Light and Life is Father-God, and from Him Man was born.

If then thou learnest that thou *art* thyself of Life and Light, and that thou [only] *happen'st* to be out of them, thou shalt return again to Life.

Thus did Man-Shepherd speak.

But tell me further, Mind of me, I cried, *how* shall *I* come to Life again—for God doth say: "The man who hath Mind in him, let him learn to know that he himself [is deathless]."

22. Have not all men then Mind?

Thou sayest well, O thou, thus speaking, I, Mind, myself am present with holy men and good, the pure and merciful, men who live piously.

[To such] my presence doth become an aid, and straightway they gain gnosis of all things and win the Father's love by their pure lives, and give Him thanks, invoking on Him blessings, and chanting hymns, intent on Him with ardent love.

And ere they give the body up unto its proper death, they turn them with disgust from its sensations, from knowledge of what things they operate. Nay, it is I, the Mind, that will not let the operations which befall the body work to their [natural] end. For, being doorkeeper, I'll close up [all] the entrances and cut the mental actions off which base and evil energies induce.

23. But to the Mind-less ones, the wicked

how doth "he who knows himself go unto Him," as God's Word [Logos] hath declared?

And I reply: the Father of the universals doth consist of Light and Life, and from Him Man was born.

Thou sayest well, [thus] speaking. Light and depraved, the envious and covetous and those who murder do and love impiety, am far off, yielding my place to the Avenging Daimon who, sharpening the fire, tormenteth him and addeth fire to fire upon him, and rusheth on him through his senses, thus rendering him the readier for transgressions of the law, so that he meets with greater torment; nor doth he ever cease to have desire for appetites inordinate, insatiately striving in the dark.

24. Well hast thou taught me all, as I desired, O Mind. And now, pray, tell me further of the nature of the Way Above as now it is [for me].

To this Man-Shepherd said: When thy material body is to be dissolved, first thou surrenderest the body by itself unto the work of change, and thus the form thou hadst doth vanish, and thou surrenderest thy way of life, void of its energy, unto the Daimon. The body's senses next pass back into their sources, becoming separate, and resurrect as energies; and passion and desire withdraw unto that nature which is void of reason.

Commentary.

The Forethought of All-Father Mind mentioned in 19 is that aspect of Mind which directs Evolution; in a word, it is the Intelligent Will which causes Nature to move in accordance with the motions of Primordial Mind; in other words, it is the Mind as the Dynamic principle engendering Kosmic Activity. Fate is the fixed trend or Norm of Evolution growing out of that Forethought. In a word, it is Forethought expressed in Action, just as Forethought is the Intelligent Norm of such Action. Harmony is here the Rhythmic Action of Fate, in a word it is the Synthesis of the activities growing out of Forethought. And it is through the united action of these three aspects, that is, through the Directive Intelligence manifesting as an Evolutionary Trend, in a synthetic Mode, that the couplings of all the diverse forms of life, differentiated as male and female, are brought about. The meaning of this is, this Kosmic Activity manifests in the particular form as a corresponding mode of energy action, which awakens their sex activity, and as this is either male or female it follows that that activity seeks its counterpart and in this way they are made to couple through the Kosmic Harmony action in the male and female form. The coupling of the male and female was the beginning of Generation, which was thus the natural outgrowth of the operation of the Harmony within the energies of the male and female forms. In this way we are to realize that the sex instinct is the natural outgrowth of the Kosmic Harmony operating through the vibration of those in whom the two sexes are separated.

This operation of the Harmony through the separated sex activity caused the multiplication of each in accordance with its kind, for the two poles of a given Species can only reproduce that which is common to them.

Inasmuch as man was not originally endowed with body, but lived above the Physical Plane, assuming a body through the accident of his misunderstanding, the self of man is applied to that

which transcends the body, while the body is
viewed not as a part of the man, but rather as
something apart from him, which he makes use
of in this physical life. To know oneself in the
sense of the true nature of man, that is, as the
original Man, will bring one into the full manifestation of that Original Man the Anthropos,
and thus will at-one him with the Good, or God-
the-Mind. It is this which is termed that Good
which doth transcend all abundance, for the reason that the abundance of all things has been projected from Mind and hence Primordial Mind
transcends all that which it hath engendered. To
know oneself as the First Man is to express Primordial Mind and be at one with the Ultimate Good.
The man on the other hand, who, through the
ordinary human love, that is, the love for a human of the opposite sex, and particularly a physical love, thus permitting love to be expended
upon the physical sensations, is led astray from
the true goal of life and remains in the physical
prison house of bodily sensations. He is in this
way shut out from the Light, and is said to stay
in Darkness wondering. This Darkness is the
Physical Life. It is darkness for the reason that
it shuts out the Light of the Higher Life, and
dooms man to live in the Phenomenal World of
Illusion. The life of the senses is therefore the
penalty for this error and there is no escape from
is so long as love is Individual and Physical.
Such a one knows nothing of a realm beyond
the Sensuous, and thinks that this is the only
life there is. He cannot form any conception of
a life above the Plane of Sensation, and for this
reason he is confined to the life of the body.
This is the real punishment for this error,
living a life bound by the Senses. Such a
one suffers through the senses things of Death,
because Death is due to a life bounded by the
senses, and it is only to the one bound by the

senses that Death applies.   Death is caused not by any Natural Law, or by Will of God, but by reason of the fact that man is bound by Sensation.   Hence it follows that Immortality is not inherent in the man living in his sensations; but by the life above the senses, the life of recognition of the True Selfhood as one with the Anthropos, is Immortality to be attained.

In 20 we are presented with the cause of Death more in detail.   Here we see the Initiation of Kosmic Thought into the causes of Death.   Death being a condition of actuality, it is bound to be due to some corresponding cause, and if we can find that cause we have found the cure for Death. The cause of Death is most clearly stated by Kosmic Thought, which indicates an awakening to the Cause of Death in the Kosmic Intelligence, and hence a promise of the elimination of this condition by the Kosmos itself in the course of time.   The gloomy Darkness is the root and base of the material frame.   From the gloomy Darkness, or Primeval Chaos, came the Moist Nature, or the Formative Power of Nature, called the Great Mother.   Thus, the Formative Principle is not of the Light, but of the Darkness of Chaos, and therefore in the Formative Activity there is not presented the element of the Light.   Out from the Formative Molding of the Moist Nature was produced the body, without the action of the Light. It is the Water, or the Moisture, that is, the Formative Activity that is resident in the body that gives it continuity; but there is at the same time present there a force of disintegration which exhausts that Formative Action, or, as is here stated, drains the Water from it, and when this Formative Action has ceased within the body, the force of disintegration overcomes the body and Death is the result.   Therefore, man having a body the product of the Moist Nature, and hence depending for its life not upon the Light, but upon the Sequence of Formation which springs from the Moist Nature, and continues in the body until overcome by the force of Disintegration, when this Formative Action is overcome, Death must result to this body, hence it abides in Death.

In 21 we are told the way in which "he who knows himself goes unto Him." The Father of the universals, that is, the Primordial Mind, the Thinking of which is the Source of all the universals, consists of Light and Life, and hence partakest not of the gloomy Darkness and the Moist Nature, and from Him was Man born, hence man is in his ultimate nature Light and Life; in a word, Man has within him a nature which is not the product of the Moist Nature, but which subsists above it. The lesson, therefore, for Man to learn is that he IS himself of Light and Life, that is to say, Life is his nature and therefore he is not dependent upon the Formative Action of the Moist Nature. In this sense man has life in himself. and not a life dependent upon the activity of any force exterior to himself. He must realize that he only HAPPENS to be out of Life and Light because of the fact that he has directed his attentions to the Universal Form, but this is not true nature. In a word, the material nature of man has been taken on by his own thought and is in no sense inherent in him. For this reason, man only HAPPENS to be out of Life and Light so long as he assumes the Formative Sphere to be his true abode. That is to say, the material realm can hold man only so long as he accepts it as being his true place. It is in reality but a voluntary exile which we have assumed, and which we can leave at any time that we resolve to do so. It is the belief that the phenomenal life is the true life of man that perpetuates that life in him, and there is nothing but belief in phenomenal existence that causes one to remain in it. When one ceases to believe in Death he returns to Life, that is, when he ceases to believe that he is a part of Nature he assumes his original functions as the expression of Light and Life.

The question, How shall I come to life again? is of the greatest importance, for up to this time we have been dealing with generalities, but now the demand is for specific directions that can be applied to the problem of one's own Spiritual Realization; it is therefore a practical question and in no sense speculative. How can one come to Life again? is the problem, for Death is an actuality and we wish to escape it; how are we to do this? If it is true that the Man who hath Mind in him is deathless, how is it that men die? This is the great question that has bothered all men for ages.

In 22 the question is, "Have not all men then Mind?" and the reply is, "I, Mind, myself am present with holy men and good, the pure and merciful, men who live piously." That is to say, the presence of Mind in one is dependent upon that one's character. In proportion to the holiness of life lived by any one will be the percentage of Mind that will be present in him. We might also say that it is the percentage of Mind in one that confers on him these very qualities. To the good the presence of Mind doth become an aid, and through its enlightening influences they gain Gnosis of all things. Now, Gnosis is not knowledge learned through the senses, but is rather that perfect knowing that dawns within one owing to the operation of the Primordial Mind within him. It is therefore, infallible in all its operations and leaves not the slightest possibility of mistake with reference to any question that it enlightens him upon. This Gnosis develops within one a purity of life that is quite Divine and hence, wins the Love of the Father, that is, there is awakened a Magnetic Affinity between the souls of such and Primordial Mind itself, so that they are brought into a closer and yet closer affinity with that Mind. The result is that all of their love is concentrated in the Mind, so that to them there is nothing else besides, and they grow into the realization of that perfect unity. They are, in fact, but the Particular Vehicles of the Mind, and its Thought is expressed in their own to the total exclusion of all other thinking. It is in this way that they become but the formal expressions of the Primordial Divine Mind.

To such men, ere they give the body up to its proper decay, that is, while they are still in the prime of their life and strength, the bodily sensations awaken a sense of disgust, due to a knowledge of what things they operate. When one has realized that death is the fruitage of sensations, one becomes disgusted with all these sensations and turns from them, clinging to the Truth which transcends all sensation. Whenever Primordial Mind is operative in any man, it opposes the mental actions that spring from bodily sensations, so that they are not permitted to work out their end. In other words, there is a dual action of mind in such a man. The Pure Mind works unto the neutralization of all the Intellectual activities springing from the Sensuous Intuitions; thus, if it be present in sufficient force it will overcome all the mentations that grow out of the senses, and one will become emancipated from the bondage of sensation unto the complete liberty of the Higher Mind. Thus it is the operation of Mind within one that liberates him from the activities of the Formative Sphere.

In 23 we are told, however, of another order of men, the Mind-less ones. That is to say, the ones who are wanting in Primordial Divine Mind, and who have only the Sense-induced Intellect to guide them. These are the wicked and depraved, the envious and covetous and those who do murder and impiety, for the reason that all of these vices are the direct result of the Sense-engendered Mind, and while they have not embodied the Primordial Mind they must in the very nature of things manifest the Fruitage of the sense-engendered mind. It is also true that so long as one yields to the pleasures of the senses he will continue to cultivate this mind and will in that way keep out the Primordial Mind, thus perpetuating his own bondage. Those who live in this way drive Mind from them, and in its place there is present that which is called the Avenging Daimon, that is, the Destructive Flame engendered by the Life of the Senses. This Daimon is the natural destruction and inflammation inherent in all sense action, the Flame of Destruction and the Fever directly engendered through the sense action; through this is he driven on to the committing of greater transgressions of the law, that is, of a still farther removal from the principles inculcated by the Mind. As a result, the man is enmeshed deeper and deeper in the life of the Senses, and he loses sight of the Light of Mind and lives entirely in the Formative Sphere or the Primeval Darkness. Thus there is continual advancement into deeper depths of Darkness, so that in course of time the man is destined to completely lose sight of the Light, and to exist only in the Formative Darkness. This process will, of course, last through several Incarnations, but sooner or later the Mind will entirely cease in him.

In 24 we enter into the study of the nature of the Way Above, or, in other words, the way in which one is to attain Mind. Inasmuch as the Material Frame or Physical Body is, by reason of the forces that have engendered it, subject to death and decay, it follows that the first step in this ascent is to deliberately surrender the body to the work of change and cease to desire its perpetuation. This comes naturally when we are persuaded that it is distinct from our self and is something that does not properly belong to us. In a word, it is an accident, a mischance and therefore, it is to be given up to the disintegrative action of the Formative Sphere. When we have ceased all effort to preserve the bodily form, it doth vanish through the disintegrative forces brought to bear upon it. Next we must surrender the way of life, that is, the habitual part of man, or, in another sense, the Karma that has been produced in the past through the life of the senses. This must be voluntarily surrendered to the Destructive Force or the Daimon, so that it ceases to be since it is no longer persisted in by us. This easily happens when we cease any longer to energize this way of life by continuing to act therein. Next, the body's senses pass back into their sources, are separated, in the sense that there is no longer a synthesis of sensation, but each particular sensation becomes separate and distinct, having no longer any affinity for any other sensation. All sensation is the result of a certain mode of energy action, hence the moment this synthetic action is broken up and all the activities made separate and distinct, that is to say, an active chaos takes the place of the ordered arrangement that was manifesting the senses, the result is that all sensation ceases and there is nothing left of the senses but the energy that was made use of as the base of the sensations. When the senses have been dissolved into energies they are no longer any part of the man, but return to the Universal Energies of the Formative Sphere, so there is no longer anything in man to correspond to the senses, they having been dissolved into Universal Energies. Thus is man made free from the senses. Passion and Desire are the positive and negative aspects of the Animal Soul or Astral Body, and when the activity which gives birth to those actions has ceased, when we neither desire nor experience passion the Animal Soul disintegrates, and flows forth as two modes of Forces of the Astral World, in this way being Astral Action, thus mingling with the Universal withdrawn into that nature that is devoid of reason; in other words, the Water has received the Water that formed the Watery nature of man, and he no longer exists as a being of either Earth or Water, for his Earthy and his Watery Principles have been dissolved into the material of which they are composed, and so his Earth returns to its Mother Earth and his Water to its Mother Water as to its source, and he ceases to be in any sense a part of Earth and Water, or nature devoid of Reason. He therefore abides in the Air, for only his Airy or Intellectual Soul remains to him, thus is he freed from Earth and Water.

SECTION V.

25. And thus it is that man doth speed his way thereafter upwards through the Harmony.

To the first zone he gives the Energy of Growth and Waning; unto the second [zone], Device of Evils [now] de-energized; unto the third, the Guile of the Desires de-energized; unto the fourth, his Domineering Arrogance, [also] de-energized; unto the fifth, Unholy Daring and the Rashness of Audacity, de-energized; unto the sixth, Striving for Wealth by Evil Means, deprived of its aggrandizement; and to the seventh zone, Ensnaring Falsehood, de-energized.

26. And then, with all the energizing of the Harmony stript from him, clothed in his proper Power, he cometh to that Nature which belongeth unto the Eighth, and there with those-that-are hymneth the Father.

They who are there welcome his coming there with joy; and he, made like to them that sojourn there, doth further hear the Powers who are above the Nature that belongs unto the Eighth, singing their songs of praise to God in language of their own.

And then they, in a band, go to the Father home; of their own selves they make surrender of themselves to Powers, and [thus] becoming Powers they are in God. This, the

good end for those who have gained Gnosis—
to be made one with God.

Why shouldst thou then delay? Must it
not be, since thou hast all received, that thou
shouldst to the worthy point the way, in order
that through thee the race of mortal kind
may by [thy] God be saved.

27. This when He'd said, Man-Shepherd
mingled with the Powers.

But, I, with thanks and blessings unto the
Father of the Universal [Powers], was freed,
full of the power He had poured into me, and
full of what He'd taught me of the nature of
the All and of the loftiest Vision.

And I began to preach to men the Beauty
of Devotion and of Gnosis:

O, ye people, earth-born folk, ye who have
given yourselves to drunkenness and sleep
and ignorance of God, be sober now, cease
from your surfeit, cease to be glamoured by
irrational sleep!

28. And when they heard, they came with
one accord. Whereon I say:

Ye earth-born folk, why have ye given up
yourselves to Death, while yet ye have the
power of sharing Deathlessness? Repent, O
ye, who walk with Error arm in arm and
make of Ignorance the sharer of your board;
get ye from out the light of Darkness, and
take your part in Deathlessness, forsake Destruction!

Commentary.

In 25 the Harmony is the harmony of the Seven

Rulers or Fires or the Seven Gucumatz, that is to say the Harmony engendered by the activities of the Great Mother or the Moist Nature. And when it is said that man doth speed his way upward through this Harmony, the meaning is that having transcended all below this sphere, the man now begins to transcend the Harmony itself, and in this way come back into the state of the Anthropos.

The seven zones are the zones of activity of the Seven Gucumatz, or the Seven Rulers, and in each zone he gives up that portion of his being that was engendered by that particular Ruler, and which he approaches in this upward flight and which is therefore, the lowest of all the seven zones and supplies the Energy of Growth and Waning. In other words, it is the activity of this Fire in the soul of man that causes the periodicity of Growth and Waning, and when he gives this up, the meaning is that he renounces all desire for growth, and the result is, that Fire that gives the periodicity of Growth and Waning ceases to operate within him, so that there is no longer Growth and Waning in the soul. In a word, he has ceased to exist in this zone, for he no longer either grows or wanes, but remains ever as he is, change has ceased for him. All Evil Devices are the result in Consciousness of the operations of the second zone, and hence, when the soul has repudiated all Evil Devices, the activity pertaining to that zone, that is the activity of that Ruler ceases to operate within the soul, and hence, he ceases to exist in the second zone. The Guile of Desires are the result in consciousness of the activity within the soul of the Energy of the third Ruler, and hence of the third zone, so when Desire has ceased, the result is the de-energizing of all the Energy previously expressed in the form of Desire, hence that Ruler has ceased to manifest himself in the soul, and one ceases to be in the third zone.

Domineering Arrogance is the result in consciousness of the activities of the Energy of the fourth Ruler, and therefore, when we have ceased to express this Arrogance we have de-energized the Energy of the Fourth Ruler, and have therefore ceased to live in the fourth zone; for us it no longer exists. The activity of the Fifth Ruler, within the soul manifests in consciousness as unholy Daring and the Rashness of Audacity, that is to say that Daring and Audacity which prompts man to oppose his will to that of the gods. When man has seen the error of his way and has given up all such Daring and Rash Audacity, the Energy of the Fifth Ruler within him is de-energized, and the result is, he no longer exists in the fifth zone. The activity within the soul of the Energy of the sixth Ruler engenders that striving after wealth at any cost and by any means. This is the origin of the Faculty of Acquisitiveness which is reflected in the organ of that name in the brain, and so when man becomes indifferent to wealth, he ceases to give expression to that form of Energy, and thus it is, so far as he is concerned, de-energized, and ceased to operate within him, and thus he ceases to exist in the sixth zone. The active energy of the Seventh or Highest of the Seven Rulers causes the soul to manifest the tendency to Falsehood, and so long as that energy is active in man, he will lie, either in thought, word or deed; but when he ceases to express Falsehood, but persists in the course of living true to all things, this energy is de-energized within him, and as a result, Falsehood becomes impossible to him. Truth becomes his very nature, and as a result the Seventh Ruler is unable to energize him; therefore, he no longer exists in the Seventh zone, and hence has transcended all of the Seven Rulers because neither of them is able to find expression in him. At this stage he is above the Harmony, and hence, in precisely the same position as was man before he broke right through the Harmony in the first place.

In 26 we are told that when all the energizings of the Harmony have been stripped from man, that is, when the Harmony no longer is able to express the workings of its Energy in the soul, and he is clothed with his proper Power, that is, the Power of one who is above the Harmony and free of all the Energies of the Seven Rulers, he cometh to that Nature which belongeth unto the Eighth. This is the Moist Nature, or the Formative Sphere, the Great Mother, which is above the Seven Gucumatz. The meaning is that now he is of the nature of the Great Mother or the Formative Sphere, and partakes of nothing below this. Those-that-are represent the activities of the Realm of Pure Formation, separate and apart from the activities of the Seven Rulers, and the meaning is that man at this stage has become identical with those Formative Activities. Here it is that he can recognize the Father, or God-the-Mind, and concentrate all of the Energies of his soul upon Him.

He becomes like those that sojourn in that Realm, in the sense that he becomes the perfect expression of the Activities of the Great Mother. Having reached this state of realization, and having purged from his soul all else, he is made capable of hearing the Powers that are above the Nature that belongeth unto the Eighth, that is, the Powers of the Ninth Sphere, or Kosmic Thought. Thus he is made conscious of those Eternal Norms of Evolution, the Processes of Kosmic Thought, which are the Eternal Archetypes mirrored in the Formative Action of the Moist Nature or the Formative Principle. He is at last able to understand the language of those Norms, that is, to grasp the Pure Kosmic Ideas, which were the Ideas that Plato spoke about. Thus the Ideal

Types of all Formation are brought within reach of his understanding, and he ceases to dwell in his Reason upon that which pertains unto the Region of the Eighth. This lifts him entirely above the Formative Sphere, and makes him a portion of the Ninth, or Ruler of the Eighth, that is to say, he becomes, through his Understanding, identical with those Kosmic Ideas or Ideal Types, and hence, one of the Eternal Norms of Evolution. This takes him out of the realm of Creative Evolution, and thus he becomes Formless, and identical with the Archetypal World of Ideas. Clothed now no longer in a Form, but clothed only in this Ideal Vesture of a Logoi, he abides in that Realm of the Logos, his life being identical with the Logos.

All those who have reached this station of Ideal Being reject all Individual Existence, and as a deliberate act of their volition give themselves up to the Powers. These Powers are the Norms of Kosmic Thought itself, the Modes of Primordial Ideation, what we might call the Categories of the Primordial Mind. By giving themselves up to those Powers, they reject all Individual existence, and become nothing other than those Divine Norms, being but Modes of Divine Thought. Thus they are not souls any longer, but merely the Active Attributes of God-the-Mind, being the diverse aspects of the Primordial Ideation and the Primordial Will or Fiat. Thus they are in God. Not gods, or Divine Beings, but so many aspects of All-Father-God. Their existence is completely lost in the Great Ocean of God-the-Mind, or Primordial Ideation, and they live henceforth as merely so many Modes of that Divine Ideation. This is the destiny of all who have gained Gnosis, that is, God-knowledge, the knowledge which comes through the Incarnation within one's consciousness of the Ideas of Primordial Ideation. This Gnosis, which is identical with the Enlighten-

ment of the Buddhists, will of itself bring man
into the realization of oneness with God-the-Mind,
not in the sense of a Human Spirit who is in
harmony with a Personal God, but rather in the
sense of the complete merging of all the Verities
in one, in the Depths of the principle of Primordial Ideation, so that he becomes merely a
Mode of Primordial Ideation, and this is identical
with the Para-Nirvana of the Buddhists. From
this it is evident that the Teaching of this entire
sermon is Pure Buddhism, and that the Hermet-
ists were the Ancient Egyptian Buddhists.

Then came the urge to Kosmic Thought to pro-
claim the truth to mortal man. Kosmic Thought
has now been impressed with the entire scheme
of Spiritual Evolution with the origin of man,
and with his destiny and also the way to come
into the realization of the same. As all this has
been manifested in Kosmic Thought, it is but
natural that it should reflect it in the Universal
Transformation and also in the humanity living
upon the earth. That is to say, the Logos should
cease to listen to the instruction of Primordial
Mind, and should instruct the Formative Mind,
through which the Harmony, and all living within
the Harmony, should be instructed.

In 27 we are told that at the conclusion of His
Instructions, Man-Shepherd mingled with the
Powers. This means that after this Illumination
of Kosmic Thought by Primordial Ideation, the
state of At-one-ment between the two ceased and
as a result, Kosmic Thought is now no longer the
pupil of Primordial Ideation, but is limited to the
Kosmos for his field of activity, thus his Ra-
tional Activities are reflected in the Universe
and in the humanity upon it. He ceases to be
the Pupil and becomes the Instructor of the Universe below him.

However, we must bear in mind that at this time Kosmic Thought is perfectly Initiated into the Mystery of Creation and Redemption as revealed to him by Primordial Ideation. It is a state of Kosmic Thought in which is perfectly Mirrored the Primordial Divine Consciousness, and not only that, but it is surcharged with the Divine Will, so that it must give expression to all that has been given to it.

This causes Kosmic Thought to manifest that which had been imparted to it, so that in all of those Kosmic Ideative activities, there was expressed the one Principle that had been imparted to Him by the Primordial Mind. This is what is meant by the Preaching to men, on the part of Kosmic Thought. This preaching simply consisted in that positive activity on the part of the Kosmic Reason, that was reflected in the Buddhi or Spiritual Souls of the people in terms of a process of reasoning which caused them to think and reason on the Beauty of Devotion and of Gnosis. That is to say, this state of the Kosmic Reason awakened in the souls of men a devotional tendency, and a thirst for the Gnosis. It was simply a trend in evolution, which engendered a Spiritual Wave of Thought and feeling and which, therefore, in a perfectly Kosmical manner drew men in the direction of the Gnosis.

The drunkenness and sleep that is deplored in this sermon was not of the physical order, but was merely that state of mind in which there is no knowledge of God, but all the faculties are engrossed with the things of sense, and there is no realization of a realm above the Harmony. Irrational Sleep is the state of the man who leads the Intellectual Life without experiencing the Pure Reason, the Mind that is governed by the phenomenal, and hence is void of the Pure Reason. In other words it is the life blinded by the

Illusion of the Senses, and the exhortation of Hermes is that they cease to be glamoured by irrational sleep, that is that they awaken their understanding, so that they will be able to penetrate the glamour caused by the sense, and see Reality. In other words, it is a plea for the exercise of the Pure Reason rather than sense engendered thought.

In 28 the gathering of the people with one accord to hear Him, simply means that this activity of Kosmic Thought penetrated the consciousness of all the people, so that their Reason was directed to the problem of those higher things, and they were through the operation of Evolutionary forces driven to the exercise of their Pure Reason and to the contemplation of the great problem.

The sermon, which was simply the awakening of the Reason within the people, and the trend which it took, called the attention of the people to the fact that Death was present in them only because they had given themselves up to it. That all their troubles were due to the fact that they were deceived by the Harmony, and if they would only look above the Harmony through the exercise of their Pure Reason they would get that understanding which would enable them to enter into Deathlessness. The sermon was therefore, merely the force of Evolution tending unto the Interior Awakening of the Pure Reason in the people.

This was not in any sense the preaching of a man to a certain number of other men, but rather the activity of the Logos awakening the Buddhi of all people, so that from within themselves they were forced to reason upon that problem which was presented to them. It was, in fact, an Evolutionary Urge in that direction, which was set up in the Reason of every man through the Active Energy of the Kosmic Reason operating within his own Reason.

SECTION VI.

29. And some of them with jests upon their lips departed [from me], abandoning themselves unto the Way of Death; others entreated to be taught, casting themselves before my feet.

But I made them arise, and I became a leader of the Race towards home, teaching the words *(Logoi)* how and in what way they shall be saved. I sowed in them the words *(Logoi)* of wisdom: of Deathless Water were they given to drink.

And when even was come and all sun's beams began to set, I bade them all give thanks to God. And when they had brought to an end the giving of their thanks each man returned to his own resting place.

30.. But I recorded in my heart Man-Shepherd's benefaction, and with my every hope fulfilled more than rejoiced. For body's sleep became soul's awakening, and closing of the eyes—true vision, pregnant with Good my silence, and the utterance of my word *(logos)* begetting of good things.

All this befell me from my Mind, that is Man-Shepherd, Word *(Logos)* of all masterhood, by whom being God-inspired I came unto the Plane of Truth. Wherefore with all my soul and strength thanksgiving give I unto Father-God.

31. Holy art Thou, O God, the universals' Father.

Holy art Thou, O God, whose Will perfects itself by means of its own Powers.

Holy art Thou, O God, who willeth to be known and art known by Thine own.

Holy art Thou, who didst by Word (Logos) make to consist the things that are.

Holy art Thou, of whom All-nature hath been made an Image.

Holy art Thou, whose Form Nature hath never made.

Holy art Thou, more powerful than all power.

Holy art Thou, transcending all pre-eminence.

Holy Thou art, Thou better than all praise.

Accept my reason's offerings pure, from soul and heart for aye stretched up to Thee, O Thou, unutterable, unspeakable, Whose Name naught but the Silence can express.

32. Give ear to me who pray that I may ne'er of Gnosis fail; [Gnosis] which is our common being's nature; and fill me with Thy Power, and with this Grace [of Thine] that I may give the Light to those in ignorance of the Race, my Brethren and Thy Sons.

For this cause I believe, and I bear witness; I go to Life and Light. Blessed art Thou, O Father. Thy Man would holy be as Thou art holy, e'en as Thou gavest him Thy full authority [to be].

COMMENTARY.

In 29 we learn that when Kosmic Thought began to manifest this aspect of Truth, there were some of the people who turned from its promptings within their own Reason, rejecting such thoughts as being the wildest nonsense, and through such rejection of the revelation of Kosmic Thought they abandoned themselves unto the Way of Death, continuing to live in the senses. Others, however, recognized the voice of Kosmic Thought in their own Reason and yielded themselves to its instruction.

As a result, Kosmic Thought became ensouled by the Reason of such men and thus led them upward, so that those who were thus ensouling Kosmic Thought became a New Race, the Race of the Logos, or the Logoi. Therefore they began the ascent towards home, that is the true station of The Man, as He was before the descent into the Harmony. This is the distinct Race of the Hermetic Souls who are on the Way of Return to the position of the Sons of The Man. On this Path of Ascent Kosmic Thought, in the Reason of each of the New Race, reveals to that one the words of Truth with reference to the Path of Restoration. In a word, it is the revelation of the Reason as to the Way. Through this illumination within the Reason of the men there was implanted within them the Deathless Water. This is not to be confused with the Moist Nature which is the Substance of Nature, but is rather the Substance of Kosmic Thought itself, that is, the Formative Mind, or the Water on the Plane of the Ninth rather than that of the Eighth. Thus there is a transmutation of the Substance into that which is of the nature of the Logos. This Logoic Water is at-oned with that of the Pure Formative Principle above the Harmony, and so they are nourished and regenerated on that Higher Plane. This is the sense in which they were permitted to drink of that Deathless Water, Deathless because it is Substance not subject to the dissolution inherent in the Formative Sphere.

The even spoken of here has no reference to the ordinary close of day, it is rather the even of their life in the Harmony. The sun is Ra or Quetzal-coatl, and the setting of the sun's beams means that in them the course of Creative Evolution was beginning to decline, as they were now passing from the realms of Universal Causation, and were entering that Region of the Eighth above the Harmony. The giving thanks unto God was the at-oning of the consciousness of these people with God-the-Mind. After this period of spiritual exaltation they returned to their own place, that is, to that state of Spiritual Attainment which had become permanent with them. In this state they were permitted to rest until such time as they were able to pass on to the Region of the Eighth as their permanent abode. This is the point of transition where man is rising above the Har-mony, but has not as yet reached the stage where he can abide permanently in the Region of the Eighth.

In 30 we are told that there was reflected in the heart of Kosmic Thought all the benefits de-rived from Man-Shepherd or Primordial Ideation, that is to say, from this time forth Kosmic Thought continued to mirror all that had been imparted to it by Primordial Ideation, so that there was a new trend to the evolution of Kosmic Thought, which was inaugurated by Primordial Mind, and which consisted in the working out in Logoic Manifestation of all that had been mir-rored in Kosmic Thought by Primordial Ideation. All that is stated in this connection indicates that the Kosmic Thought was the perfect mirror of Primordial Ideation. In a word, Kosmic Thought was perfectly Initiated into the First Mystery, and the evolution of this epoch was the effort of Kosmic Thought to impress this truth upon the Evolving Universe and its Humanity.

We are informed that this was the results of All-Father-Mind being reflected in Kosmic Thought. As a result of this God-inspiration, Kosmic Mind came into the Plane of Truth, that is to say, it was the perfect mirror of Primordial Ideation or Bodhi, as the Buddhists would say. As a result of this Initiation Kosmic Thought reflected itself in the Universe and in all of its activities reflected the Mind of the Father, and this was the sense in which it was uplifted in His Praise. In other words, it was no longer operating on its former level but was expressing the truth of the Primordial Mind.

In 31 we have the elements of this recognition and praise of the Mind. It is to be borne in mind that the expression "Holy art Thou" is repeated nine times, and Kosmic Thought is the Region of the Ninth, which means that all the forces of Kosmic Thought are taken up in the expression of Primordial Ideation.

The first recognition, "Holy art Thou, O God, the universals' Father," is the recognition that all of the universal principles operating in evolution are but the activities of the Norms that are the manifestations of Primordial Ideation. That is, there is not any evolutionary principle which is not the mirroring in Nature of the Ideation of God-the-Mind. Therefore there is no such thing as Creation, but there is merely the mirroring of Primordial Ideation in the Forces of Creative Evolution. Hence there is no line of demarcation between God and Nature, but a continuous sequence of activity from Primordial Ideation through all the manifestations of the Evolving Sequence which we call Nature.

In the second statement, "Holy art Thou, O God, whose Will perfects itself by means of its own Powers," we are informed that the Will of God, which is merely the Active Potency, or centrifugal activity of Primordial Ideation, is perfected, that is, reaches its consummation through the Powers of Itself, that is, through the expression of the faculties of Primordial Mind in terms of their own Centrifugality or Will, which is expressed in terms of Evolutionary Modes of Action.

In the third realization we are told that God Willeth to be known, and is known, by His own, that is to say, the Will of Primordial Ideation is made manifest in the Modes of Divine Expression, that is, Norms of Evolution are the active modes of the Will of Primordial Ideation, in which Primordial Ideation is revealed.

In the fourth realization it is seen that Primordial Ideation did through its Word, or Will made manifest in Reason, engender all that is, that is to say, the order in evolution is the manifestation through Reason of the Thought of the Divine.

In the fifth realization we are told that All-nature has been made in an Image of Primordial Ideation. The meaning of this is the Primordial Ideation has been mirrored in the Universal Substance, and as a result, Substance has reflected Divine Ideation, thus becoming a Kosmos, that is, the Active Evolving Image of Primordial Ideation. Hence, God did not create the Universe as He pleased, but rather His own Nature was reflected in Kosmos so as to reproduce itself in Evolutionary Modes.

In the sixth realization it is stated that Nature never made the Form of God. The meaning of this is that Primordial Ideation has not been Evolved from Nature, and also that Nature has never realized the Form of Primordial Ideation, but has merely reflected it on a lower plane, thus Nature has reflected a Picture of God, but has not realized the Form of God.

In the seventh realization it is seen that while all the Powers of the Universe are the reflection of the Power of Primordial Ideation, yet they are all together unequal to that Primordial Power. In other words, while the Manifest God is the manifestation of the Unmanifest, yet the Pleroma of the Unmanifest is not expressed in the manifestation so as to make of the manifestation the equal of the Unmanifest. Or, from another point of view, God is in Nature, but that God in Nature is inferior to the God above Nature.

In the eighth realization we are shown that Primordial Ideation transcends all the pre-eminence of the Universe, that is to say, all the pre-eminent Powers of the Universe are but the reflection of the yet Higher Power or Primordial Ideation, which, though reflected in them, is greater in itself than in its reflection.

In the ninth realization it is seen that no amount of praise on the part of either man or nature can do justice to the grandeur of God-the-Mind.

Next we have the rendering of the reason of Kosmic Thought as an offering to Primordial Ideation, which means that during this cycle of evolution Kosmic Thought is permanently at-oned with Primordial Ideation and gives forth the perfect reflection of It in all of its operations. Naught but the Silence can express the Name of Primordial Ideation, for nothing can realize through speech or activity the depths of that Great Verity, hence we can only be still and permit it to manifest in our Consciousness. Words will not express it, neither can we express its fullness in our thought, but can only reflect it. No one can describe Primordial Ideation, though it can be mirrored in our Consciousness.

In 32 Kosmic Thought becomes negative to Primordial Ideation to the end that it may never of Gnosis fail. Gnosis is the knowledge which comes from Primordial Ideation, and therefore it can only be mirrored in Kosmic Thought through the Thought of Primordial Ideation. Hence the longing on the part of Kosmic Thought is that it may ever reflect the perfection of the Gnosis of the Primordial Mind in all of its activities. It longs to be filled with the Power or Will of God-the-Mind, unto the end that through its own activities it may reflect the Light of the Father in such a way that all of the Race of the Logos, that is, the ones rising above the Harmony who are yet in ignorance of the true nature of the Gnosis, and in this way they may rise to the region of the Ninth, where they will be the Brethren of Kosmic Thought as being of His own Nature, but the Sons of Primordial Ideation as not having as yet arisen to His Level.

In the last paragraph we pass from the Kosmic Reason or Hermes, and come to those of the race who have reached the Region of the Ninth. They affirm their true destiny to be the Life and Light of Primordial Ideation, and affirm that their aspiration is to come into the status of the Archetypal Man, who was the perfect Image of His Sire, and hence in every sense of the word the exact duplicate of God-the-Mind. This means the return to the status of the Anthropos as the Image of All-Father-Mind as it was when first projected into being. And we are told that this is the destiny of man, and that he has full authority of the Father to return to this status. This is the state from whence he descended in the process of incarnation, and to this he is to return in the course of his evolution. This return to the status of the Anthropos, is the Plan of Salvation as laid down in the Hermetic teaching. But the most important feature of this sermon is not so much the fact that man may reach the status of The Man, but that Kosmic Thought has begun a course of evolution in the Universe, the direct effect of which is sooner or later to bring mankind into that state, not through his own efforts alone, but through the regular course of Creative Evolution as a Kosmic process. Therefore there is nothing that can prevent the ultimate return of humanity to that status of the Anthropos, or the Image of Primordial Ideation. In Buddhist parlance this would mean that the end of Creative Evolution was the exaltation of all humanity into Nirvana. This is undoubtedly the teaching of the Mahayana, and this shows that it was not an innovation when introduced in the Orient, but that it was known in the time of Hermes Trismegistus, and had been a fundamental Hermetic doctrine for thousands of years before the time of Buddha.

The Shepherd of Men

PART TWO

The Origin of Civilization

CHAPTER ONE

THE ATLANTEANS

After the Great Upheaval which brought to an end the Third or Lemurian Race, the next manifestation of Life and Consciousness was on the Continent of Atlantis. This Land and the Race that inhabited it have been known by different names at different times and in different countries, but whether it is spoken of as the Land of Moo, the Country of the Mud Hills, the Sacred Lands, or the Land of the Ethiopes it at all times means the same land and the same people. Homer speaks of the land far beyond the setting Sun, beyond the Pillars of Hercules, where the Ethiopes dwell, and it is Atlantis that he has in mind. The question then is, why does he call these people the Ethiopes? The term Ethiopes has two meanings. In the first place it is the Bright Faces or the Shining Faces, and in the second place it is the people who spoke the language of Ether, or Aether, according as we use the Greek or the Latin spelling. There are two kinds of Ethiopes known to the Ancients. There were the Mythical Ethiopes as they are sometimes spoken of, though they were not Mythical at all, for they were the Lemurians, and then there were the Historical Ethiopes or the Atlanteans. These latter spoke the language of Aether, that is the original Lemurian Language, and therefore were an outgrowth of that Race who were the same as the Giants who were destroyed by the Thunderbolts of Zeus. They were called the Bright Faces or the Shining Faces because of their peculiar complexion.

The original Atlantis was not a continent but

was rather a low plain that connected North America and Europe, so that there was but one continent. At that time the Sahara Desert and also the Gobi Desert were covered by the Sea, and the same was true of a great portion of North America. The great center of human life was Atlantis. The people who lived upon it were a very Spiritual and Idealistic race. This was the time indicated by the Greeks in their traditions of the Golden Age.

The First Sub-Race of the Atlantean Root Race was very Spiritual indeed. They were the Yellow-White or Moon Colored Race. In the course of time they developed a more dominant and slightly less Spiritual Sub-Race, the second in the series, who were of a pure Golden complexion. This was the Ancient Golden Hued Race, the Lords of the Sacred Fire Principle. This was in reality the Golden Age of Song and Verse. During their reign Philosophy was at its height. After the lapse of time, this Golden Hued Race gave way to a more material Race, who were the Third Sub-Race of the Atlantean Root Race. This Race was of a Red complexion, and were the Red Atlanteans. They were the Race who specialized Science until it reached a height such as it has never attained at any other time, either before or since. Not only were the Physical Sciences reduced to an absolute Unity, but they delved into Occult Science to a degree that has never been equaled since their time. They were the Incarnations of the Pure Fire Principle in its Material Aspect, and the result was that they were the absolute masters of the Hermetic Fire. This people were the Hermetic Scientists par excellence. Their Civilization was the organized expression of Hermetic Science in all the relations of manifesting life. In course of time, however, they turned their attention from Speculative Occultism to Practical Occultism, and this in time led to their degeneracy. From Hermetic Science they turned to Hermetic Art, that is, the majority of them did, and, of course, the inevitable result of giving their attention to Practical Occultism was manifested in their lives. They became material and practical, and developed into a lower type. This lower type was called the Black Race, though they were not in reality Black, but Dark Red while the Red Atlanteans or Third Race were of a very Bright Red complexion. Thus was born the Fourth Sub-Race or the Dark Atlanteans. They were merely the evolution out of the Third or Red Atlantean Race. They turned to Magic and Alchemy, and finally to all forms of Psychism as well. They developed the war spirit to a very high degree and almost conquered the entire world. Naturally their Magical and Occult practices degenerated into the Dark Side, until, about the time of the sinking of the country, they were a race addicted to the higher forms of Black Magic.

As time went on the Red Race became numerically weaker and the Dark Race numerically stronger, until at last the entire country was dominated by the Dark Race.

During all this time the form of government had remained largely the same, that is to say it was a union of the Theocratic and the Autocratic form. The basis of one's standing in the Aristocracy was his degree of Initiation, and his resultant Spiritual Attainment. The Emperor was at all times the Highest Initiate and for that reason was in a sense the Head of the Hierarchy. His position as head of the nation caused the Union of the Sacerdotal and Political functions in his person. There was, however, a balance in the power owing to the fact that the actual functions of the High Priesthood were not discharged by the Emperor but by the High Priest. The fact, however, that the High Priest was of necessity a member of the

Royal Family caused him and the Emperor to act in harmony. Another arrangement which worked for the balance of power between the two was the fact that the Emperor was the Spiritual subject of the High Priest, while the High Priest was the Political subject of the Emperor.

As time went by the Land of Atlantis gradually sank below the surface of the Ocean. In this way the Continent of Atlantis was formed by the sinking of that portion of the land that connected it with what is now North America, and also with Europe. The British Isles being the highest part of the country remained above the water and thus the Isles were separated from the Mainland of Atlantis and also from Europe. The people who were inhabiting them at the time of the separation from the mainland remained upon them, and their descendants became the Celtic Druids. The original Religion of the Druids was that of Atlantis, though in time it degenerated to some extent. The wonderful civilization of the ancient Druids was therefore the survival of the Atlantean Civilization.

The land continued to sink from time to time, and at last there was nothing left but the Island of Poseidonis, which stretched from Greenland to the Azores Islands, and was fifteen hundred miles from East to West. In time this was entirely dominated by the Dark Atlanteans, they having driven the Red Atlanteans out of the country long before. Some time before this the two Races became so distinct that they formed two distinct Nations, the Red Atlanteans being known as the White Empire, owing to the fact that they had nothing to do with Black Magic; they were the Bright Faces or the Shining Faces, and their Nobility were called the Lords of the Shining Face. Their Emperor was at all times spoken of as the White Emperor, because he was the Head of the

White Adepts, or the Adepts of the Sacred Art.
The Dark Atlanteans were called the Black Empire, for the reason that Black Magic was the
fundamental Principle of their entire organization, and their Emperor was called the Black Emperor, for he was the Head of the Black Adepts
or Adepts of the Infernal Art. They were so
much addicted to the Dark side of the Art that
the Nobles were called the Lords of the Dark
Face. These two Empires were in the fiercest
antagonism at all times, and at last the White Emperor and all his followers were forced out of
Poseidonis and driven to North America. In this
way the Black Emperor became supreme on the
island, and it was entirely given over to the
practices of the Dark School. From this, however, it must not be assumed that they were
a savage people. On the other hand they
were from the standpoint of modern utilitarianism far more highly civilized than any
Atlantean People had ever been before. They
were a more material people and for that reason
turned their attention to the accomplishment of
material results. In that way they developed a
very Material Civilization, that is, a very Utilitarian one. It is natural in a Spiritual Civilization
for the people to attach little importance to material conveniences, but to bring all the powers
of their being to bear upon the attainment of the
Spiritual Attributes, while in a material civilization just the reverse is the case; they do not consider the Spiritual Attributes, or even Philosophical knowledge, of any value except as it yields
material results. Of course the Poseidonian
Civilization was somewhat inconsistent from the
standpoint of modern material civilization. It will
be difficult for our materialists at this date to conceive of a civilization where Utilitarianism had
reached its highest possible development; where
aerial navigation had been reduced to an absolute

science, and aeroplanes were used for the conveyance of freight and passengers from one end of the Island to the other and were run on regular schedule, the same as railroad trains are at the present time; where Electricity was the crudest power known to man, and was only used for the purposes for which Steam is now employed, while for all high pressure work a still more subtle force was made use of. The pure Ether, the Odic Force, the Astral Light and some yet finer forces were harnessed in this way and were made practical use of in the Mechanical activities of life. Their knowledge of Applied Mechanics, Physics, and Chemistry was far in advance of all the dreams of the Modern Mystics. While this will all appeal to the Materialist, he will be surprised to learn that this same people were Alchemists and Astrologers, and that they developed some of the Psychical Powers to a tremendous degree. Telepathy was developed to such an extent that the official spies of the Government depended upon it as a means of detecting rebellion, and the police made use of it as a means of locating and preventing crime. The Judges made use of it to detect perjury in the witnesses, and in fact all the relations of life were determined by the telepathic information that one might receive. Also Hypnotism was developed to a tremendous degree, and the Nobles and the Priesthood controlled the people, not through fear of temporal or spiritual chastisements, as in the case of other peoples, but through force of Will, in other words the People were kept in a state of semi-hypnotic subjection to the ruling class. This, of course, made them more and more subjective, and caused their downfall, while at the same time this abuse of Occult Power on the part of the ruling classes was the means of their downfall also.

At last after a very long period of this accentuation of the Material side of an Occult Civilization, the Forces of Disintegration became so great that the Earth itself was disturbed and in time there was a great Catastrophe—so great as to cause the entire Island, that last remnant of Atlantis, with the exception of America, the British Isles and some unimportant islands, to sink below the surface of the Ocean—and the mighty Atlantic rolled peacefully over the Land of Moo, the Country of the Mud Hills. In one Night it went down with its sixty-five millions of inhabitants. Some of them escaped in their air ships and others in boats, but the refugees were only a few thousand, while the vast hordes of the population went down in the terrible destruction. This was a little more than eleven thousand years ago. For several thousand years the mud was so deep where the Island had stood and the ocean was rendered so shallow that no ships were able to cross and for that reason it was not possible for the Eastern Continent to have any communication with America, and thus it was that the two remaining Continents were entirely isolated from each other and all knowledge the one of the other ceased. Thus was ended the ancient grandeur of Atlantis save as it was perpetuated among the Atlantean peoples who had previously migrated to the American Coast. Among them the two warring factions continued until the King of the Golden Gate was forced from the City of the Golden Gate down into Mexico, where the descendants of the White Atlanteans are to be found to this day.

What is the lesson taught us by the Fall of Atlantis? It is this, Occultism is not an Art to be practised for the purpose of accomplishing Utilitarian results, but rather it is a Philosophy to be studied for the purpose of bringing oneself into the closest possible unity with the Creative Force of Evolving Life. Anyone who fails to understand this truth, will be sure to start on the downward road which will lead to destruction. Progress is only possible when we are working in accord with the Constructive Principle of Nature; if we work against it, degeneracy is inevitable.

CHAPTER II

THE MAYAS

In the latter days of the Red Atlanteans and the first days of the Black Atlanteans, or, to speak more accurately, in the time of transition, when the Black Race was being developed from the Red Race, some 3,000 years before the sinking of Poseidonis, or about 13,000 years B. C., there took place a great migration of Red Atlanteans from Atlantis to Yucatan. These people were the pure Red Atlantean stock. All were Initiates of the Hermetic Brotherhood and of the Mystery of the Feathered Serpent. This was while the Island of Atlantis was still standing and at the time of the sinking of the mainland of the Continent of Atlantis. These people were not only Initiates of the Mystery of the Feathered Serpent, but also into the Mystery of the Great Mother. They were the original stock of the Atlantis of that time, two former Sub-Races having disappeared. Because of this fact they claimed to be the Mother Race, from which the Black Atlanteans were derived, hence they took the name Mayas. Ma means the womb, esoterically the Womb of the Great Mother, hence Mayas means the Womb People or the Mother Race. Esoterically this means they were the original Race of that time and also that they were the Womb of the Mexican Races; that is, the Mother of Nations. Esoterically it means they were the embodiment of the Great Mother Principle. They were the nation that was organized on that principle. They gave to their country the name of Mayax, or Mayach, which means the Womb Land, or the Mother Land. This was due to the fact that this land was the Cradle of Mexican Civilization and also of the Civilization of the Orient. Colonies sent out from Mayax established the Civilizations of Egypt and of Asia.

The ruins of Chichin Itza and other cities of Yucatan bear witness to their grandeur and the extent of their Civilization. They did not attain to the beauty and the sublimity of Civilization that was reached later on by the Toltecs, nevertheless they were far superior to any civilized nation of the present day.

We know of their great antiquity for the reason that the Mastodon was their National Totem. Now, a Tribe of Indians never chooses an Animal as their Totem unless they are familiar with it, but, once chosen, they are tenacious of all such Symbols and are never likely to change it for something else. This being the case, it is evident that a Tribe would never choose an extinct animal as their Tribal Totem. This leads to the conviction that the Mayas would never select the Mastodon as their Totem if it was an extinct animal, or even a rare one, at the time; hence they chose it at the time when it was common in Yucatan. This proves that at the time the Mayas came to Yucatan there were Mastodons all over the country.

In the main they perpetuated the Civilization of the Red Atlanteans of that time, though, of course, this went through a period and a process of Evolution among them. They lost sight of some of the elements of Red Atlantean Civilization and developed some features that were unknown to their Red Atlantean Ancestors. The foundation of their Educational System was Geometry, Mathematics, Astronomy and Astrology. They also practised Augury and Divination. Perhaps the element in their Science that will interest the modern mind the most was their Biological System. They were Darwinians 14,000 years before Darwin's time. They believed that Man was evolved from the Ape. This was known not only from their History and the Tradition that has survived from them, but also from their Hieroglyphics. Their language was simply a modified form of that of Atlantis. Their Sacred Hieroglyphics were derived from the Totems and the Sacred Animals that were the Celestial Correspondences of those Totems, and also from the Geometrical glyphs. Mayan was the Ancient Sacred Language of the Initiates in Accadia, Babylon, Persia, India and Egypt. In course of time it was lost in the most of those countries, but there are Adepts in the fastnesses of Thibet, and in the Gobi Desert, who still are in possession of this Sacred Language, which is simply the Ancient Mayan Tongue. For evidence as to this aspect of the problem, presented in such a manner as to appeal to the Scientific mind, the reader is referred to the invaluable researches of the late lamented Dr. Le Plongeon, who accumulated enough to convince any one but an Archaeologist of the truth of his position. It is not the mission of the present writer to go into those details, but rather to give the Mystic Key to the problem, so that his readers may have the advantage of the Esoteric Tradition, and may see the truth from the standpoint of an Initiate of the Temple. This knowledge cannot be had except from one having the Inner Knowledge which will give the Key to the Symbols.

One of the most peculiar features of the Mayan Civilization was the Gyneocracy, or government by women. This can only be understood when we realize that with the Mayas the Great Mother was the most important of all the Gods or Goddesses. It is true that in the Brotherhood there was recognition of the Heart of Heaven and also of the Feathered Serpent, but above all these conceptions rose that of the Father and the Mother of the Gods. But in this arrangement the Mother of the Gods was far the most important. The entire nation was in reality the organized expression of the Cultus of the Great Mother. For this reason we are to look for this conception of Motherhood cropping out everywhere. Mayax was to all intents and purposes the Mother of every one of the Mayas, and for this reason we may look for a situation in which the Royal Family is recognized as the Mother of the People. This was, indeed, the fact, and yet the Sovereign was the King and not the Queen, as one would have supposed would be the case under the circumstances. Also, we do not find the idea of succession through the female line rather than the male line as we might have expected. However, this does not so much matter for the reason that the Mayas were monogamous, and as the King had but one wife, the children would succeed through both the male and the female line. The peculiarity of the arrangement of succession was the fact that the Youngest Son of the King was the Crown Prince and succeeded to the throne. There was another peculiarity in the arrangement and that was the Crown Prince was at all times married to his Oldest Sister. Thus we have the peculiarity of the marriage of the Oldest Daughter and the Youngest Son of the King. As a rule, therefore, the King's Wife was at least twenty years older than he was. While he was yet a boy, the Crown Prince was married to a woman who was approaching middle age. This arrangement will become clear when we realize the purpose of it. The King's wife was at all times old enough to be his mother, and she was in reality in loco parentis to him. She acted as a sort of Foster Mother to her husband. The Mayas seemed to hold to the idea that it was the duty of the wife to mother her husband, and so they married the young King to a woman who would be enough older than he was that she would naturally mother him, and also that he would accept the mothering as a matter of course. Furthermore, it is customary for the older sister to in a manner bring up her younger sisters and brothers, and they get used to obeying her, and in many instances are disciplined by her; now, it was assumed that the Eldest Daughter of the King would as a matter of course act as a sort of second mother to her Little Brother, and that he would get so used to obeying her and listening to her advice that he would naturally continue to do so after they were married. Now, inasmuch as the foundation of all Maya social life was the Feminine element, they grew to look upon the woman, as the embodiment of that principle, as being a safer guide than the man, and therefore they assumed that it would be better for a man to be under obedience to some woman than to follow his own inclinations, and if he must be guided by any woman, who was better for this function than his wife? As all were under the guidance of the Great Mother, it followed that the human mother was the proper interpreter of that Great Mother while she lived, and after her death the man's wife as his second mother was to fill that function. After the marriage, the King was supposed to obey his Sister-Wife, and therefore she exercised the real rule over the country. She did not come to the front before the people, but rather ruled her Brother-Husband in the home and molded his character. Thus we have the practical application of an idea which is held by many at the present time, viz., the wife is the interior or Spiritual Expression of the Family, and as such the inspiration of her husband, who gives expression in an outward way to that which is given him by his wife. The Queen, as the expression of the Divine Mother, was therefore recognized as the Guide of the King, who merely interpreted her will to the

people in his official conduct. What the Queen was
to the King, so in a less degree was the wife to the
husband throughout the entire nation. In every instance the wife was the head of the husband so
far as the Inward Principles were concerned,
though the husband was the visible head of the
family. We might express this matter in other
terms by saying that the husband was the formal
head of the family, while the wife was the real
head of her husband. We do not find so much
difference in this arrangement and what is in practical operation in a great many families at the
present time, with this exception, that, whereas,
in the present day the husband assumes to be
the head of his wife and she therefore has to rule
him through diplomacy, in the Maya family life
she was recognized by all, the husband included,
as his Spiritual Director. The real relationship
might best be indicated by saying that the wife
exercised pretty much the same influence over
her husband that the Confessor exercises over a
Catholic. She was, in fact, his Confessor and
Spiritual Adviser. It was for her to reveal the
Law to him, for was not she the natural mirror
of the Great Mother, and were not all subject to
the Great Mother in every thing? The obedience
of the husband to his wife was, therefore, in reality obedience to the manifestation of the Great
Mother. It was therefore outwardly that the
husband was the head of his house, in reality he
was subject to his wife, as the Power behind the
Throne, who guided and disciplined her husband,
who was little more than her mouthpiece, while
she was both the Heart and the Directing Intelligence of the Household.

From the foregoing it will appear that the
Maya regime was a Feminism in almost every
particular. At the same time it must be borne in
mind that no woman actually filled any office.

That was the work of man; her function was to
rule her particular man. There was one thing,
however, that redeemed the Mayan Civilization
from complete Feminism. This was the Priesthood. The Elder Brother of the King and Queen
was at all times the High Priest. He was therefore the natural Guide and Director of both of
them, and as the Interpreter of the Will of the
Gods he must be implicitly obeyed by all, even
the Queen herself. As he never married, but remained a Celibate, it followed that he was not
under Feminine influence or control, and therefore he was able to bring a perfectly free Masculine intelligence to bear upon all. Therefore we
see a situation which has never been duplicated
in any other country, the Elder Brother-High
Priest was the Head, the Elder Sister-Queen was
the Heart, and the Younger Brother-King was the
Hand of the nation, or perhaps we might better
call him the Mouth of the Hierarchy. From another point of view they were the visible expression of the Heart of Heaven, for the High Priest
was the Heart that Thinks, the Queen was the
Mouth that Speaks, and the King was the Eyes
that See. In this sense the Priest was the Vehicle
of Thought, the Queen of Word, and the King of
Deed. In the family the Priesthood represented
Thought, the Wife Word and the Husband Deed.

CHAPTER III

THE AKKADIANS.

The first colony to be established by the Mayas was that of Akkad. In the very beginning of Maya Civilization, only a short time after the landing of the Mayas in Yucatan and long before the sinking of Poseidonis, a party of Missionaries set out from Mayach. The mission was one of Education, Religion and Commerce. The Mayas being an aggressive and conquering race, they sought expansion in every direction. They came to the coast of Western Asia. A party of explorers sailed along the coast of the Indian Ocean to the Persian Gulf and thence up to its head. There seven of them landed under the command of Oannes (he who dwells on the water). However, we must not make the mistake of taking this in too literal a sense. The fact that they were commanded by Oannes simply means they were a seafaring people, and as the natives of the country were dwellers on the land they would give the name Oannes to any people who came from over the seas. Also the number 7 is rather suspicious. This is one of the most sacred numbers to the Mayas and to all other Mystical Peoples, and hence we are justified in looking for a mystical meaning in the number. Seven being the number of completion, we are to understand that this was a thoroughly equipped colony that settled here. They had with them an organized Priesthood, a Civil Government and an Educational system, as well as a thorough Commercial establishment. This party of Colonists went ashore and were the first Maya Colonists to land on Asiatic Soil. The landing was made at the mouth of the Tigris.

They ascended that river to its confluence with the Euphrates. Entering that river, they followed its course of about sixty-five miles and founded their first settlement in the marshy lands, to which, on account of the nature of the soil, they gave the name Akal, a Maya word meaning swamp or marsh. In the course of time this word became altered to Akkad, and therefore the name Akkadians was given to the dwellers in the marshy lands at the mouth of the Euphrates. These details, or the most important of them, are also to be found in the work of Berosus.

They surrounded their settlement with a palisade of reeds for protection against the lions that abounded in those marshes, and also for defense against the aborigines of the alluvial plains of Mesopotamia. Their settlement thus enclosed they called "the enclosed place," or Kalti, from the Maya "kal" (enclosed) and "ti" (place). In course of time the aborigines, changing the "t" into a "d," called them Kaldi, by which nickname their tribe continued to be known in after times, when as Caldeans they became numerous and powerful, having acquired great influence through their learning.

In a short time after the establishment of this settlement there were several thousand other Mayas who came here and settled, and in time the city of Akkad or Akal became a great emporium for ships, which traded with all the outlying countries, and thus in time it became the greatest maritime center in all the Eastern Hemishpere. In this way was built up a great Commercial Empire, the seat of which was Akkad. In time this city dominated all of what was later known as Lower Chaldea. This city was in fact the capital of the entire country and became the favorite burial place for all those anywhere near. It is now known as Mugheir. In their tombs they used the pointed triangular arches which were used in Mayach, and which characterize Mayan Civilization wherever it may be found. Not only was this true of the construction of the tombs, but the position of the bodies was identically the same as that in which they were placed in Yucatan. Loftus, "Chaldae and Susiana," page 134, gives this description, which is quite accurate, of the position of the bodies: "The body was laid upon the matting. It was commonly turned upon its left side, the right arm falling toward the left and the fingers resting upon the edge of a copper bowl, usually placed in the palm of the left hand." To understand the significance of this practice we must bear in mind that the Mayas placed the body on the left side, with the right hand resting on the left shoulder, if he were a man of some distinction. The bowl was the symbol of the vase, which was supposed to contain the man's good deeds. It was in fact, what Theosophists would call the receptacle of the Man's Karma that was to go over to his use in the after death state and also in future births. This vase for the reception of the man's good deeds was the measure of his justification, and hence it was the Vase of Justification. Among the Mayas it was resting on the stomach or rather the abdomen, in many cases. Among the Akkadians the bowl resting in the palm of the left hand symbolized the fact that one carries his good deeds into the after state with him, and that it is on the basis of his good deeds that his future status is to be determined. From this it is to be seen that they did not believe there was any forgiveness of sins, but rather that one must earn salvation for himself.

The settlement of Akkad having become a town, is was called Hur, from the Moon Goddess, which was the principal Divinity worshiped by the inhabitants. King Uruk raised a temple to her honor, which is an almost exact fac-simile of the temple erected to the God of the Sea, and also as a royal archive, at Chichen.

Hur grew to be a great center of Religion as well as of Commerce and Science, and it was here that the real Akkadian Civilization centered. In the later Centers of Life they were merging more toward the Chaldean or Babylonian Civilization, which was in reality nothing more than another and later development of that of the Akkadians.

The second capital of the Akkadians was situated twenty-five miles from Hur in a northwestern direction, on the east side of the Euphrates and about eight miles from its banks. This was built by King Urukh. The name of this city was Lallak, "lal" (companion) and "lak" (rude)— "the rude companion." In time the spelling of this name was changed from the Maya to the vernacular form and the result was the name became Larrak.

Some fifteen miles from Larrak, to the northwest and on the same side of the Euphrates, was built the Sacred City, where dwelt the God Anu and his wife Ishtar, and her Priestesses, the sacred courtesans. This city, sacred to Anu and Ishtar, was at first called Uruk from the name of its builder. Later it was changed into Erech and later into Warka.

Sixty-five miles from Uruk, on the east side of the Euphrates, thirty miles from its bank, on the edge of the Affej marshes, midway between that river and the Tigris, was erected the last great city of the Akkadians. This was Nibpul, "nib" (offering) and "ppul" (jar); that is, "the place where offerings of jars are made." The God Bel was the principal Divinity of this place and offerings of jars were made to him. This city flourished more than seven thousand years before Christ. Since that time it has been destroyed and four

super-imposed cities have been built above its
ruins, each one being built over the ruins of the
one below it.

There was in Nippur a most extensive library,
for some twenty-three thousand baked-clay tab-
lets have been recovered from it. This library
was situated in the Temple of Bel. There were
also a great number of very valuable works of
art, only a few of which have been recovered so
far.

The city had the most improved methods of
sanitation, equal to the best in Europe or America at the present time. They made use of the
keystone arch and many other modern improve-
ments.

Blue was the mourning color of these people.
This is proven by the fact that many of the
coffins still have a coating of blue glaze upon them.
As blue was the mourning color of the Mayas,
this is of great value as a proof that they were
the same people as the Mayas.

Nippur was the seat of Akkadian Culture until
the Akkadians were gradually transformed into
the Chaldeans and erected the city of Babylon. Being Mayas in their descent, they preserved to
a great extent the Maya system of government
and society, though in the course of time the Feminism of the Mayas disappeared from among
them, to give place to a more masculine form of
society. Nevertheless, it was from these Akkadians that the primitive Feminine impulse was
derived which exercised so much influence over
the ancient Orient. They were a Poetical and
hence a Symbolic people, and therefore their
form of government was based upon the Mystical
Symbolism they had brought with them from Mayach. At the same time we are to bear in mind
that their Civilization, partaking largely of the

Utilitarian form, was destined to cause them to lose sight of the more Spiritual element they had held in Mayach. One point, however, which is well for us to bear in mind is this—their form of government was a Theocracy. The real rulers of the country were the Gods. There was a Celestial Hierarchy that ruled in the Heavens, and this Celestial Hierarchy had its counterpart in the Terrestrial Hierarchy that ruled as their correspondent upon earth. From time to time their Theology underwent changes, so that first one, then another, God or Goddess had ascendance over the others, and the color of the Celestial Hierarchy was changed accordingly. This being the case, the Terrestrial Hierarchy was of necessity bound to change accordingly. This was the real reason why the government was never stable in its constitution. The King ruled as the Vizier of the Supreme God, and was His servant to do His Will. This being the case, there was never a permanent constitution to the country, for the Supreme Law of the Land, was the Will of the Divine Hierarch, who ruled the Gods as expressed through the King as His Hand and the High Priest as His Mouth Piece. As the God who ruled the Heavenly Hierarchy was not at all times the same, it followed that the complexion of the government changed that of the Celestial Hierarchy recognized by the Ruling Class. In many countries there is a definite principle which is universally accepted as the foundation of government, and any government that falls short of this principle has forfeited its right to exist. However, among the Akkadians this was not the case. The supreme law was the Will of the Gods. At the same time there was no definite authority among the Gods, first one and then the other was in the ascendancy. Now it was the duty of the King to express the Will of one of the gods above that of all the others it was

at the head of the Hierarchy at that particular
time. When the King established the Cultus of
one of the gods above that of all the others it was
assumed that that god had gained ascendancy
over the others, and that the King was acting
under his direction when he placed that Cultus
above all the others. At the same time every
one of the gods had His own particular nature;
that is to say, an individuality of His own, and
therefore the government must take particular
tone when He ruled in the heavens. It was this
principle which led to so many apparent contra-
dictions in the form of government. It was the
duty of the King to see that all served the gods
and particularly the Chief God. Each city had
its own Patron God, and for that reason when a
city became the capital of the country its God
was recognized as being the head of the Hierarchy, for if this were not the case how could it be
that His city was at the head of all the cities in
the nation? This becomes clear when we realize
that Akkad was a Sacred Land, ruled absolutely
by the gods, and, further, that its government
and its geography were patterned absolutely after the heavens. The entire idea underlying
the Akkadian system was to form on earth an
exact counterpart of the Heavenly Hierarchy,
and all of its Laws and Customs were derived
from this idea and founded upon this laudable am-
bition. Of course the practical working out of
this system was the placing of absolute and un-
questioned power in the hands of the King.

Much of the Archaeological information contained in this article is to be found in The Word,
issue of May, 1913, article "Origin of the Egyptians," by Dr. Le Plongeon, and all our readers
are urged to procure the magazine and read
that article. The author has made some use of
said articles in procuring data for this contribu-

tion to the Maya History. However, the other matters, dealing as they do with the Inner Life of the Akkadians, are drawn from the Secret Archives of the Hermetic Brotherhood and are authentic in every detail.

CHAPTER IV

THE CHALDEANS.

The Akkadians in the course of time sent out
many parties for the purpose of founding settle-
ments. One of these parties came into Upper
Chaldea from the East by the way of the country
of Shinar, that is, Lower Chaldea, or Akkad,
and were strangers in the land into which they entered, that is, Upper Chaldea. See Genesis—xi:2.
They settled on the right bank of the Euphrates,
65 miles from Nippur, and there built the ancient city of Borsippa. Here they erected a high
mound, called to this day Birs-i-Nimrud. This
mound is the exact fac-simile of the great mound
at Izamul, which was dedicated to Queen Moo,
who was Atlantis, and the Red Atlantean Religion
also, as shown in a former editorial in Temple
Talks. She was worshiped here as the Goddess
Kinich-kak-Mo, even down to the time of the Span-
ish conquest. The mound on which the Tower of
Babel stood and the mound of Kinich-kak-Moo are
identical in their forms, and this goes to show that
the mound of Kinich-kak-Moo was the original
which was copied in the construction of the mound
of Borsippa. On this latter mound was erected
the Tower of the Seven Lights of Earth; hence
it was erected to the Great Macaw or Vukub-
Cakix, the Mayan Hephaistos, in its double-sexed aspect. This was the famous Tower of Babel.
This word Babel is derived from two Maya prim-
itives—BA, ancestor, and BEL, the way—meaning "the style in which our ancestors used to
build." Then there is a mystical meaning to
the name also, for BEL is "the way" in the
sense of being the Course of Nature and in that

sense became the name of the Feathered Serpent, as the Evolving Universe, or the process of Creative Evolution which constitutes the Universe. In this sense it was dedicated to the God of our ancestors. And this indicates that they were Mayas in every sense of the word. They not only preserved the same style of Architecture but had also the same religion as the Mayas. For while the mound on which this tower rested was dedicated to Vukub-Cakix, the tower itself was dedicated to the Feathered Serpent or Bel. This proves beyond a doubt that the first settlers in Borsippa were Mayas. The city of Borsippa was built around the base of the tower, and for a time was the seat of the Chaldeans who had come here. At a later date the city was removed some 12 miles farther north, and was then called Calah, from CAH, town, city, and LA, the Eternal Truth, God, the Sun, hence Bel or the Feathered Serpent, the Way; therefore it became known to foreigners as "The City of the Lord," of Bel or Belus. By the Greeks it was called Babylon. After the building of Calah, Borsippa became the residence of the Chaldean priests, and became, therefore, the seat of Chaldean Sacred Learning, just as Hur was that of the Akkadians. In the course of time, the Chaldeans became so powerful as to completely absorb the Akkadians, so that Akkad and Chaldea became one country, as they had all the time been of the same Race. This led to a new development of Religion and Philosophy and a new type of Civilization, so that a new type of humanity was evolved, thus making of the Chaldeans a new type evolved out of the former Akkadians.

Among the Chaldeans the king was the high priest, whose title Rab-Mag, is but a slight transformation of the Mayan spelling of the word LAB-MAC, the old man, the venerable. The title of the Mayan high priest was HACH-MAC, the true, the very man, i. e., the Archetype. To understand the meaning of this we must take into consideration a very profound Hermetic doctrine, that of the First Man, or the Anthropos. According to this conception, the Original Man was not as we have him now, but was the very image of All-Father Mind, or Primordial Ideation; he was even above the Logos, or Thoth, and was, in fact, the Perfect Image of His Sire. He was also Male-Female in the state of perfect balance. In time he descended into Incarnation, and became the human man as we see him, or rather as the First Race were. However, this First Man is held up as the Perfect Archetype of Humanity, and as the state to which all must return in the course of the Evolving Cycles of Time. This First Man is the True, the Very Man. Hach-Mac, the high priest, is supposed to be the type on earth of this First Man, and to be the Vehicle through which He is made manifest on earth. Again, LAB-MAC, when used mystically, means the old or the venerable man, in the sense of the First or Archetypal man. When the king as high priest is called Rab-Mag the meaning is that he is assumed to be the type on earth and the vehicle for the Archetypal or First Man. See ''The Origin of the Egyptians,'' by Le Plongeon in The Word, Vol. 17, No. 2; also Le Plongeon's ''Sacred Mysteries Among the Mayas and the Quiches,'' pp. 30-45, where much data will be found on the above details.

The most important of the Chaldean gods were Ishtar and Bel or Belus, hence their Religion was a development of that of the Akkadians.

However, we do not find the Anthropos conception among the Akkadians, and therefore we see in the Chaldeans this important departure from the former system. Also there was another distinction, and that was in the great attention paid to Astrology and Magic. Bel was supposed to be the Course of Creative Evolution going on in the Universe, and this was supposed to manifest itself through certain differentiations or Modes, each of which manifested itself through one of the Stars, and in this sense the Stars were supposed to be the channels through which Bel operated, and hence the Rulers of the Process of Creative Evolution among Men. Having accepted this view of the matter, it followed that the Stars constituted a sort of Intermediary Hierarchy between the gods and the earth, and that it was through their intermediation that Bel ruled the earth, and hence humanity. Human Evolution was supposed to be regulated by the motion of these Heavenly Bodies, hence all Cyclic changes were produced by them and could be indicated by their movements. To know the forces in human evolution it was only necessary to reduce the motions of the Stars to a system. This gave rise to the Science of Astrology. Chaldea was a Sacred Land that was modeled after the motion of the Stars. In fact the government was designed as the Political Pattern of the Stellar Hierarchy, being patterned after it in every detail.

The rays of the Sun, and hence the physical action of Bel, coming in contact with the Earth, caused the springing forth of Vegetation; thus the cultivation of the soil became the direction of physical evolution. This gave rise to the idea that the direction of human evolution would be a sort of Spiritual Agriculture. This system was developed along Astrological Lines, and formed a perfect Science of Soul Culture from the Astrological standpoint. This system was called the Nabathean Agriculture. It was the systematic Culture of Souls in accordance with the Astrological influences, which were supposed to rule all the motions of the Magnetic Principle in its effects upon Life and Consciousness. The Educational System of the country was regulated in accordance with this Nabathean Agriculture. Nabathean Agriculture is of great interest because of the light which it throws upon the general concept of the Chaldeans. They did not recognize individual ideas in any sense whatsoever when it came to Education. Their position was that there was a definite course of Evolution going on in the Universe, and that humanity was being slowly evolved in accordance with that process. It was therefore desirable that the people should be evolved in accordance with that type which was to be ultimately realized. In a word, there was a Goal toward which all their efforts were to be directed, and every feature of organized society must tend to the production of that type. Thus far we presume all will agree that this ideal was most desirable. However, the problem is ever present as to what the Goal may be. In a Popular Government, the educational system and the Public Policy of the Government are ever subject to change, and with the evolution of the people, and a Monarchy, it would be assumed that the private opinion of the king would determine the policy and the educational system of the time, but this was never the case in Chaldea, for the reason that there was no question as to the Goal of Education. The Nabathean Agriculture was accepted as an Exact Science. Although the king was an Absolute Monarch, he never dreamed of calling in question the Nabathean Agriculture any more than a king at the present time would think of questioning the fundamental principles of Mathematics. The Nabathean Agriculture was supposed to give the last word in the true method of Education, and no man ever thought of wishing any other type of man than what its principles would produce if followed. This science

of Soul Culture was, therefore, the basis of every
system of Education ever attempted in the country. Thus it was that there was never any doubt
as to the type of humanity that was to be realized
in the nation. As the Nabathean Agriculture was
the systematic application of the principles of
Astrology to the Culture of Souls, it followed that
the only way it could be changed was to make
a discovery in Astrology that would show that
some of its principles were not in accordance
with the Laws of Astrology. The practical workings of this system was that the Astrologers actually dictated the policy of the king, for it was
the Astrologers who furnished the data for the
Nabathean Agriculture. Chaldea was therefore
the first nation to formulate what was accepted
as an Absolute Science of Sociology, albeit a
Science founded upon Astrology, which Sociology
determined the Laws of the Nation, although
those Laws were proclaimed by an Absolute
Despot. Therefore, we have the peculiar situation where the king had the power to slay an
Astrologer at will and yet dared not enact a Law
which Astrologers declared to be out of harmony
with Astrology, for in order for a Law to be Legal
it must be a means of carrying into effect the
Principles of the Nabathean Agriculture. Of
course, in a country organized upon such a basis
as this there could be no room for individual in-
itiative and the development of individual pecu-
liarities, for every Chaldean had his entire life
ruled by the Principles of Astrology from the
cradle to the grave. The entire policy of the
government was regulated by the desire to realize a common type of humanity, and every other
consideration had to be set aside for the realization of that end.

Here we have the theory that the Individual
must be sacrificed to the common good worked

out to the ultimate limit. For instance, it was held that there was nothing so desirable as the increase of the population to the ultimate limit, and to insure this end it was desirable that all the women should have husbands, but there were some of the women who were so much more desirable than others. This difficulty was obviated by reason of the fact that no woman had anything to say in the selection of her husband. The women were sold at public auction, each going to the highest bidder as long as a man would pay anything for her. Those for whom no one would pay were then given away, and when all were taken that anyone would have on that basis they began to give premiums with each one, giving her to the one who required the smallest bounty with her, thus the auction went on until all the undesirable women had been disposed of and had carried with them in the form of premiums all the money that had been paid for the most desirable ones, and in this way all were married, and at the same time the desirable women had in reality bought husbands for their less desirable sisters. To those who look upon love as a sentiment this sale of women will seem abominable, but such must realize that to the Chaldean marriage was but a means of insuring the perpetuation of the Race. This is but an illustration of the universal system operating among this people, the object of which was to evolve a civilization in which man was not an individual, but a cog in the great machine. The whole being dominated by Astrology and Magic, for the government was but the Socialized aspect of Astrology and Magic. The Religious intolerance of the Chaldeans is easily understood when we understand that Astrology depended for its Sacredness upon the worship of Bel, or the Universe. Were a people to introduce a Religion the god of which was not subject to Bel, i. e., was supposed to be

above the Universe, and to govern things independent of it, the will of such god would be
stronger than the Universe and hence the influence of the Stars would not apply in that case.
The result would be, there would be another rule
of conduct than that indicated by the Stars, and
that would mean the setting aside of the Nabathean Agriculture. As all the laws of the kingdom were derived from the principles of the Nabathean Agriculture, to call in question the Nabathean Agriculture was to dispute the authority on which the Laws rested, and thus to over-
throw the established order, hence all who worshiped any god who was supposed to be able to
dispense with the influence of the stars and to
overcome them were in fact Anarchists, and were
dealt with accordingly. For this reason, they
were perfectly tolerant of any Religion the god
of which was under the authority of Bel, but absolutely intolerant of all who claimed for their
god equality with or superiority to Bel, and this
intolerance was not Theological but Political and
Sociological, for the Bel worship was the foundation on which the entire fabric of Society rested.
All who look upon Astrology as being a true Science will see the value of this arrangement.

CHAPTER V

THE EGYPTIANS.

There are two elements that must be taken into consideration when we come to deal with the ancient Egyptian Race. There was, first of all, a people who were very slightly civilized, who came North from Lybia and Aethiopa, and settled in Egypt in Prehistoric times. This Race knew nothing about the art of weaving and dressed in skins of animals worn around the waist. They were a primitive people, though not savages at the time they entered the valley of the Nile. It is from this people that we have evidences of a primitive state of culture.

However, in 11,800 B. C. there came a party of Chaldean Mayas into Egypt and settled in the valley of the Nile, forcing their superior Civilization upon the Aborigines and introducing their Religion into the country. From this people Egyptian Culture was derived. The Egyptian Race proper was the result of amalgamation of the two Races. Soon after the coming of the first settlers from Chaldea into the country there came great hordes of immigrants from Mayach and also from Atlantis, who settled there and augmented the colony, so that in less than a thousand years there were more of the Mayan Stock in the country than there were of the Aborigines. This led to entire transformation of the Civic Structure as well as of Religion, manners and customs, though many of the original customs continued over into a later period. For instance, the Egyptian Apron that was always worn by the common people was the survival of the original skin worn around the waist. But the barbarous manners and customs gradually yielded to the superior culture of the Mayan invaders, and in time there was little left of the original type. The two types in the course of a few thousand years were completely merged into one, the Egyptian, and all the people claimed descent from Mayach.

When the Mayas came from Chaldea they settled on the banks of the Nile, and gave to their settlement the name of MAIA; that is the same as MAYA with the Y changed into I, which indicates that they were Mayas who wished to give their new home the name of the Land of their Ancestors. The idea was that in Maia they were founding another Mayach. These people at all times claimed their ancestors came from the West, that is, from America, and they had a hieroglyph to represent their ancestral birthplace; it was a rough draft of the Yucatan peninsula, the seat of the Mayan Empire. They adopted a system of burial similar to that of the Mayas, that is to say, in mausoleums with a pointed arch roof, which shows they were preserving the ancient Mayan system in this respect.

At the time of the coming of the first Mayan settlers, those from Chaldea, a large portion of Egypt was covered with water and the explorers had to travel in boats. For this reason they gave to the entire country the name of CHEM, the Mayan name for boat, hence CHEM, the Land of Boats. They traveled along the shores of the desert, and called it XUL-END, meaning that this was the end of their journey and that they were going to settle here.

The Mayas coming into Chem brought with them their language and the Sacred Hieroglyphics and introduced then into the country. This Sacred Language flourished until the sinking of

Atlantis rendered the Atlantic Ocean so shallow that is was no longer possible for ships to cross it, and in this way communication was cut off between Egyptians and the Mayas of the West. This was 9,600 B. C., 2,200 years after the settlement of the Mayas in the country. As a result of this separation of the people from their Motherland in Mayach the Sacred Language was in time lost, and so the Second Thoth, we are told, translated the ancient writings out of the Sacred Language into the Egyptian Tongue, but still used the Sacred Hieroglyphics. In this way was perpetuated the ancient Books of Thoth, which were originally written in the Sacred Language or Mayan, but which were not translated into Egyptian, as the Egyptians no longer understood the Sacred Mayan.

Egypt was made a Sacred Land of the Mayas. It was designed to be the mundane pattern of the Universe and particularly of the heavens. There was the Celestial Nile or the Sacred River, which ran through the Upper and the Lower Heaven. This Upper and Lower Heaven were the Two Planes of Super-Physical Existence and the Sacred Nile was the Mystical Stream that connected the two Heavens. In other words, it was the Stream of Force that flowed from the Upper Heaven into the Lower Heaven, the Emanation of the Lower Heaven from the Upper Heaven, in fact. To understand this, we must bear in mind that the Lower Heaven was the Astral and Etheric Region, the place of Fabrication, the place of all Physical Formation, from which the solid earth and all bodies are produced; it is also the Great Green, or the Waters of Space, and the Pool of Pant, or the Place of Torture; it is the Womb of the Earth Fabrication. The Upper Heaven is the Formative Sphere in the Higher Kosmical sense of the term and the Heavenly

Waters of the Great Mother, also the Realm of Fire; in a word, it is the Kosmic Substance from which all things in the Universe have proceeded. This Celestial Nile, flowing from the Upper to the Lower Heaven, is therefore the course of Emanation from the Formative Sphere to the Fabricative Sphere just above the earth. The Nile was the symbol of this Celestial Nile, and so was Upper Egypt the Symbol of the Upper Heaven, and Lower Egypt of the Lower Heaven. The 36 Nomes of Egypt corresponded to the 36 Decans of the Heavens, for Egypt was the Universe to all intents and purposes. Ra was the Universe, and so the King was the Son of Ra, that is, the son in the sense of the Visible Incarnation of the Universe. Hence he was crowned with the Double Crown of the Upper and the Lower Land or the Upper and the Lower Heaven. Therefore the King was Divine in every sense of the word. The Red Sea became the Pool of Pant, for Egypt was the world, and the Pool of Pant was the Etheric Boundary of the World.

The Totems of the Mayas became the foundation of the Egyptian Hieroglyphics, and as many of the Totems were not in existence there, they had to select the Animals that most nearly correspond to them or to the ideas which they represented, and in this way the Egyptian Sacred Animals were developed.

The Calendar of the Mayan Egyptians was always Solar, though there was an earlier Lunar Calendar and also a still earlier Stellar Calendar among the Lybians who inhabited the country befor the Mayan invasion.

The system of Society among the first Egyptian race was an absolute Feminism, because their religion was that of the Great Mother, who had no husband, the Old Generatrix, or Kaf. While the Mayas had a Feminism, it was not so exaggerated as that of the Lybians who inhabited Egypt before them; neither was it so crude. With the introduction of the Sun Cultus or the Cultus of the Feathered Serpent, and that of the Father and Mother of the Gods and also of the Heart of Heaven, there was introduced into Egyptian Thought a more philosophical element, which was soon reflected in the form of Society and thus there was a great change introduced into Egypt.

The Religious Rites of Egypt present a peculiar mixture of the Ancient Rites of the Lybian element and of the Mayas. For this reason we find the greatest difficulty in distinguishing between the two, and yet we will never understand Egypt unless we do. All the crudities and the Sensuous element come from the Lybians, while all the Philosophy and Transcendental Metaphysics found in Egyptian Sacred Writings come from the Mayas. For a detailed discussion of the former element in Egyptian Antiquities see the writings of Gerald Massy, and for much valuable information about the Mayan element see Le Plongeon—"The Origin of the Egyptians" and "Queen Moo and the Egyptian Sphinx."

One peculiarity about the Egyptian Religion is the fact that under Mayan influence it became so very philisophical that the gods frequently change places and are used interchangeably, although each has a different meaning, and thus it is somewhat difficult at all times to distinguish just what is indicated. Another thing which must never be lost sight of is that the Mayans to a great extent accepted the system of the Lybian Barbarians and made use of it as a system of symbolism to represent their own Philosophy, and this Dual Element makes it sometimes difficult to distinguish between the Apotheosis of Lybian Superstition and a pure form of that Superstition that may have survived. We must never lose sight of the fact that in Egypt we have two distinct elements, a Barbarous people and a people of the Highest Culture that the world has known, and that these two elements and bloods became perfectly fused into a common stock, which became the Egyptians of history.

CHAPTER VI.

THE NAGAS.

At the same time that the Mayas settled in Akkad there were other exploring parties that set out for the coasts of Asia. One of these parties, however, sailed westward by way of the Pacific ocean, hence they came from the western portion of Mexico, at a time shortly before the first beginnings of the mighty Toltec race. At this time the Mayas had covered practically all of Mexico and Central America, and as they wished to extend their dominion they sought other countries, and, being the rulers of the sea, they struck right across the Pacific. This was some 13,000 B. C. After a long voyage, lasting for several years, during which they visited several of the islands of the Pacific and established colonies in a great many of them, a portion of the party reached the Dekkan Peninsula, where they established a small settlement. In later times, this settlement became the mighty Naga Empire. They conquered and settled the whole of what in later times was called Hindustan. They gave to themselves the name of Nagas, meaning Snakes, which shows that they were worshippers of the Guchumatz and of Quetzalcoatl. Their king went by the title of Khan. The Nagas extended their conquests westward and northwestward, until the entire territory of southern and western Asia was dominated by them as far as the Akkadian and Chaldean Empire. They settled Burmah and Ceylon, and covered all India and Farther India. We are told in the Ramayana, Hippolite Fauche's Translation, Vol. 1, page 353, that their coming into the country was in times so remote that the Sun had not risen, but we are to bear in mind that the Hindoos had not been in India previous to about 5000 years ago, and hence the Nagas had been there 10,000 years before they came, hence their great antiquity would appeal very strongly to the barbarous Aryans. Their remains are to this day quite visible in Java, where they settled, and left great architectural evidences of their residence. All of those buildings are the exact duplicates in point of style of those in Yucatan, and thus we see the indisputable evidences that the civilization of ancient Java was that of the Nagas.

They extended their sway westward, and settled what is now Afghanistan, Turkestan, Beloochistan, as well as all Persia. The Afghans are their descendants. In 1879 there were Maya tribes speaking the Maya language residing on the banks of the Kabul river, a name which in Mayan means the Miraculous Hand. Throughout all of that section of Asia the major portion of the ancient place names that are still on the map are pure Mayan names, having a distinct meaning in the common language of the Mayas, but being only place names in other languages. For a list of those names and their meaning in Mayan, see the Word, Vol. XVII, No. 1, article, The Origin of the Egyptians, Le Plongeon. All India and Persia and the adjacent countries were dominated by the Nagas, and their great culture spread throughout all southern and western Asia. In the course of time their dominion became so great that it was unwieldy, and in time it was divided into the Southern and Western Empire, though they were the same people. The Southern Empire comprised all India, Burmah, Ceylon, Java Afghanistan and adjacent countries, while the Western Empire comprised Persia and the adjacent territories as far as Akkadia and Chaldea.

Among all the Nagas there was the same form of government; the king was divine, and ruled as the Son of the Sun or of the Great Serpent. He was the visible incarnation on earth of the Divine Power that was identical with Quetzalcoatl. Hence his power was absolute and was to be called in question by no one. Not only was the king divine, but there was a measure of Divinity attached to the persons of all in whom flowed the royal blood. In Persia the doctrine that whatever the king willed was right, was the outgrowth of the ancient belief that he was divine. That the Serpent or Sun God was manifest in him, and hence his will was but the individualized form of the Divine Will. Also, the Mind of the God was manifest in his mind, and hence all his decisions were infallible, hence all the decrees that he made were infallible, and as they in reality emanated from the Mind of the Serpent God they were as changeless as He was, therefore the decree of a king could never be changed, for it had come from the God, and the God did not change his Mind. Thus it was that while the king was infallible and all powerful, yet he could not in the slightest degree alter any of the decrees of his predecessors. The laws of the country were merely the body of the decrees of all past kings.

In the course of time human sacrifices became introduced among the Nagas, both those in India and also those in Persia. There is a legend of one of the Persian kings, who had a snake growing out of each of his shoulders, and that these snakes had to be fed every day on the hearts of men, and as they grew there was an ever increasing number of human hearts that had to be given to them, so that the country groaned under the scourge. At last there was an uprising, in which the king was killed and a new king set up in his place. The meaning of this story is not hard to discover. The king was the dynasty at that time. The snakes were the cultus of the Guchumatz and of Quetzalcoatl. Their growing out of the shoulders of the king indicated that the ruling dynasty was devoted to the worship of those deities, and that the royalty was directly connected with the priesthood of the Cultus. The feeding of the hearts of men to the snakes indicates that according to the Cultus at that time these Serpent Gods had to be propitiated with human sacrifice, and that it was only the hearts that were sacrificed to them. Thus it is that we see the necessity for a great number of victims for the altars of those deties. But the question is, Why did they offer the hearts to them in preference to any other portion of the victim? The answer is not difficult to discover. The heart was by many of the Maya nations believed to be the seat of the soul, and the idea was that the Serpent Deities devoured the souls of men. This gruesome Cultus is still surviving in the Shiva Cultus of India, which is the direct survival of the Indian Nagas. Then there was another reason for this practice, the heart is the seat of the emotional nature, and this belongs to the domain of Quetzalcoatl. It is a fundamental Hermetic Doctrine that as one ascends toward his source he must give up the emotions and all the Astral activities, or de-energize those energies, and in this way permit them to return to their source in Quetzalcoatl, and there is no doubt that this sacrifice of the hearts of men was designed to symbolize the interior sacrifice which every man must make of his emotional nature. There grew up in the course of time the idea that inasmuch as the de-energizing of the Astral energies caused them to return into the great supply or Quetzalcoatl, he was nourished thereby, and hence, would suffer if he was not fed regularly in this way. We see identically the same idea current among

the Aztec barbarians in Mexico when they adopted
the Quezalcoatl Cultus. In the course of time
the Nagas reached the conclusion that the sacrifice
of the hearts of men would of itself de-energize
the Astral energies, and we must bear in mind
that this belief is the origin of the practice of
cremation, and that the Hindoos and the Buddhists of the Orient believe in it at the present
time. This may be disputed at first, but it can
very easily be proven. They think that so long
as the body continues, the Astral will be bound to
the earth, and that the soul can never reincarnate,
and as reincarnation takes place only upon the
de-energizing of the Astral Shell it follows that
they cremate in order to de-energize the body and
let the Astral go free, and in time it will also
become de-energized. The practise of cremation
was introduced by the Nagas for the purpose of
de-energizing the body, and facilitating the de-
energizing of the Astral, not out of tenderness
for the dead, but in order that Quetzalcoatl might
be nourished upon those energies as they returned
to Him, and the practice of cremation has ever
since been the direct survival of that superstition. Now, all this being true, it followed
that if the energies of a dead man were good to
eat, those of a live man were better, and so they
adopted the custom of offering the hearts of men
to the God. Then there grew out of this the idea
that this sacrifice would operate vicariously for
the living, and hence we have the complete Cultus of Human Sacrifice. Of course, the longer
the Cultus stood the more victims were required,
and in the end the toll became unbearable and
there was a revolution in which that dynasty was
overthrown and the Cultus brought to an end.
The practise of human sacrifice was ended and
there was a reformation in the Cultus of Quetzalcoatl and the Guchumatz and they were restored
back to something like their original form.

It was, however, those sanguinary rites and the beliefs associated with them, that formed the sanguinary character of both the Persian and Indian Nagas, and that have survived through their descendants with but few exceptions. Notwithstanding this, however, they were one of the most highly civilized peoples that the world has ever known.

CHAPTER VII

THE ARYAN INVASION.

Five thousand years ago there was a party of Ayran Barbarians who left their Bactrian home and entered India. They first entered the Punjab and there established their home on the banks of the Saraswati, then a tributary to the Indus. From the time of their first arrival, these barbarians began a war of conquest on the cultured and spiritual Nagas. These were the barbarians who later on became the Hindoos, a race that has ever been characterized by its barbarism, falsehood, materialism and mental mediocrity, and, above all things, its religious intolerance.

At the time of their entry into India these barbarians had no religion aside from the crude form of Nature Worship and the practice of Magic. Their first gods were Varuna, who meant Space; Duyas, who meant the Bright Sky, and Rudra, who meant the Sun. However, we must not make the mistake of assuming that Rudra was the same as Quetzalcoatl or Ra. The latter was the Universe in its metaphysical aspect, as the process of Creative Evolution, of which the Sun was merely the symbol, and he was never the Sun, but at all times The Man of the Sun, when conceived in the solar sense. The Aryan Barbarians were not far enough evolved to conceive of anything so abstract as this metaphysical conception, and to them Rudra was the physical Sun as the giver of light to the world. Their Trinity was, therefore, Space as the Source of all Activity, the Sun as the Vehicle of Light, and the Bright Sky as the physical manifestation of the Light diffused by the Sun. From this it is to be seen that they worshiped physical Light and nothing higher than this. As Light and Fire are very closely connected, these primitive people conceived of Agni or Fire as the other pole of Light, that is, activity of Rudra manifested not only as Visibility, but also as Heat. However, we must not make the mistake of assuming that they had the conception of Divine Fire. This Fire was purely physical, though they did have the conception of the latent fire in space, which was manifested as the visible fire. Again they conceived of this Fire in Nature manifesting as Indra, the Lightning, or Celestial electricity. There was also the personification of the Four Elements, one of which was Agni. The Maruts or Storm Winds were also supposed to be the atmospheric reflection of an etheric principle, so that the Maruts were worshiped as gods. The Light was also supposed to differentiate itself into diverse forces, some of which acted creatively, and were called Devas, or Bright Ones, that is, Lights; and others which worked destructively and were called Asuras, which later on became the Devils. Through the process of personification which is characteristic of all barbarous peoples these Devas and Asuras became the basis of a sort of Fairy lore, and the above is all the religion that the Aryans had previous to their contacting the highly civilized Nagas. At the same time it is to be borne in mind that they conceived of the Moon as the feminine counterpart of the Sun, and to it was given the name of Soma, and the Soma worship was nothing more or less than the adoration of Moon Light as the gestative principle of the Earth Life. Also they worshipped Death, under the name of Yama.

If thou shouldst listen to the modern descendants of those Aryan Barbarians they will make thee believe that the Vedas are the embodiment of all wisdom, past, present and to come. Just what are the Vedas? The Rig Veda is the ritual for the worship of these mundane gods; the second Veda is the ritual for the Soma sacrifice, that is, the sacrifice to deified Moon Shine; the Yajur Veda, or the third of these holy Vedas, is the ritual for the working of practical magic; and the fourth, or Atharva Veda, is the ritual of black magic. The religious observances of the Aryans consisted entirely in the practice of magic, and the more magic power one had, irrespective of how he obtained it, or what he did with it, the greater was the measure of his saintliness. Austerities were universally practiced, not for the overcoming of the carnal instincts, as they were by some of the philosophical Nagas, but frankly for the obtaining of supernormal powers in a magical sense. The result was the development of Tapas, or the practice of austerities as a means of acquiring powers which were to be used for the gratification of the vanity of the Yogi who possessed them. Out of Tapas grew the idea of Vedic Karma, or the acquiring of merit through ritual observation, which frankly meant the wonder working power of magic, which would enable the Ascetic to dominate the gods, and as they were merely mundane forces, this was quite possible to the trained mind and will. These saints were merely the devotees of natural and ceremonial magic, and that is the only religion taught in the Vedas, all claims of Hindoo liars to the contrary notwithstanding.

These barbarians came in contact with the highly cultured Nagas and in the course of time the Naga influence was manifested in their religion until in the course of time there was developed a very philosophical religion, the tenets of which are to be found in the Upanishads. Their leader who brought them into India, who is the historical background of the myth of Manu, devised a system of Laws that are the origin of the Laws of Manu and the adoption of that Code was the first step in the direction of Civilization.

Shortly after their entrance into India they began a relentless war on the civilized Nagas. After this war had gone on for a time Rama appeared upon the scene. Rama was the spiritual leader of the Aryans, who for the first time introduced Ethics into their philosophy of life. Previous to his epoch, they thought of nothing but Vedic Karma, but from this time they began to accept the validity of a moral life in theory, though they have never put it into practice. We have some very quaint statements in the Ramayana which will bear observation. It will be well here to try and fix the period of Rama. He was born at the time of the Horse Sacrifice. The Horse in the Indian Zollac is the same as the Lamb in others; that is, it is the sign of Aries. The Horse Sacrifice was to celebrate the Vernal Equinox in Aries. This occurred 2433 B. C., and hence the period of Rama was some time subsequent to that date. This would place him some 600 years after the Aryan invasion, if not later still. We are told that Rama broke into the lime light as a protector of the Rishis. That is to say, when they went to sacrifice to the gods, the devils assailed them, and scattered the sacrifices and the fire in every direction, so that they could not succeed in making the Sacrifice. At last one of them called upon Rama to come to their aid. He went and in the first encounter slew several of the devils and dispersed the rest! Now what do you know about that? The idea of one man killing several devils and dispersing a whole crowd of them single handed! The facts in the case are, those devils were men. They were fanatical Nagas who were enraged at the heathen rites of the Aryan Shaman, and determined to prevent the sacrifice. In plain language, they were a mob of over zealous partisans of the true religion. Rama being a soldier and well armed, and as these zealots were not armed, he butchered a considerable number of them, and the rest fled for their lives. This is the inside of that devil killing on the part of Rama. They were called devils by the Aryan Barbarians because they were the enemies of their Heathen rites.

The whole of the Ramayana is nothing more nor less than a history of the war of extermination which Rama and his barbarian host waged against the cultured Nagas in Ceylon. Ravena was not a devil, but a man, and the Naga King of Ceylon. It is very singular that a devil should become enamored of a woman! But quite plausible that a man who was an Oriental Despot should fall in love with her and should see no reason why he should not take unto himself the wife of a Barbarian and a Heathen. Hanuman, the Monkey King, was simply the king of a tribe of Aryans who had the Monkey as their Totem, and his army was the Monkey Gens of the Aryans. He was not in reality a king at all, but simply the head of that Gens. The bigotry of the barbarians as usual caused them to multiply this war over the possession of a woman into a religious war between the Incarnation of God and the King of the Devils, but, stripped of all its trappings, the above is exactly what took place.

After a time a much more spiritual condition was entered upon by the Aryans. They grew and, overcoming the Nagas, plagiarized their civilization without mercy. Finally we come down to the time of Krishna. By this time the barbarians had conquered enough of the Naga territory to have contacted the culture of the peace-

ful Nagas, and to have incorporated a great deal
of it.   We have now the development of the
Vishnu Cultus.   Vishnu was the direct plagiariza-
tion of the Heart of Heaven, at least as the Heart
that Thinks, Primordial Ideation.   Also the
Buddha doctrine was plagiarized and transformed
into the doctrine of the Avatars of Vishnu.   The
Trinity of the Heart that Thinks, the Mouth that
Speaks and the Eyes that See was changed into
the Trimurti of Brahma the Creator, Shiva the
Destroyer and Vishnu the Preserver.   This was,
of course, the corruption of the original doctrine,
as the true Trinity is not the three aspects of a
Principle all on one level, but rather the manifestation of one and the same Principle on three
levels.   Durga was made the Consort of Shiva,
and in this way was elevated to the spiritual
plane, and thus losing all of her Kosmic meaning was in the course of time transformed into
Kali, the Bloody Mother.   Thus, that which had
at one time been a Kosmic truth became in time
a spiritual ideal.   However, down to the epoch
of Krishna, Vedic Karma held full sway, although
ethical conduct was recognized as desirable from
the time of Rama.

The work of Krishna was twofold.   He lived
in the time of the Great War, which had already
been raging for over a thousand years, and therefore he sided with his people, the Aryan Barbarians, and aided in the crushing out of the last
remnant of the Naga power.   He was also at
war with the Naga religion, and with Arjuna
waged relentless war upon the Quetzalcoatl Cultus.   It is that stage of the war that was going
on at the time that the Bhagavad Gita was written.   Krishna was also engaged in the reformation of the Aryan religion.   His breaking the
bow of Rudra was in reality the abolishing of
the Cultus of Sun Worship.   There is in reality

a very great deal of history in the Mahabharata and the Puranas if one can dig it out from the mass of mythology. It is the history of the conquest of the philosophic Nagas by the Aryan Barbarians, and the final incorporation of the Naga Civilization into the Hindoo superstitions, which was in reality the means of giving a real religion to those barbarians, and also of making a Civilized people out of them. After the amalgamation of the two races and the confusion of the Naga religion and civilization with the barbarism of the Aryans there began a period of real culture for the Aryans, which period developed the body of Upanishad literature. Krishna in reality marked the beginning of religion among the Aryan Hindoos, and about a thousand years before the age of Buddha Sakyamuni they had become a civilized people.

Shortly after the Aryan Hindoos invaded the Naga kingdom of India the Iranians came down from their Bosnian home and invaded the Naga kingdom of Persia, where, after a long period of time, they succeeded to a great extent in dominating the Nagas. But the Sakya clan, both in India and Persia, have in the majority of cases preserved their Naga blood from contamination by any intermixture with that of the Aryan Barbarians down even to the present time.